April 15-21-1999

THE TIMES TRAVEL LIBRARY

Edited by Paul Zach

Times Editions, 422 Thomson Road, Singapore
© Copyright by Times Editions 1988

Printed in Singapore by Koon Wah Printing Pte. Ltd.
Color separated by Daiichi, Singapore
Typeset by Superskill Graphics, Singapore

Cover: An East Kalimantan beauty, dressed up in
her festive gear, at the popular Erau Festival. Once
held annually, the Festival is now held every two or
three years, attracting villagers from the length of
the Mahakam River.
Endpapers: The Mahakam River is the lifeblood of
East Kalimantan. The rivers of Kalimantan, as
Borneo is now known, have always been the
avenues of travel and trade inside this huge island.
Frontispiece: These trading boats anchor off the
Kalimantan coast, much as they have done for
centuries. Sail is still the dominant means of
transport between the islands of Indonesia, a vast
archipelago which stretches from the Indian Ocean
to New Guinea.

ISBN: 981 204 000 5

EAST KALIMANTAN

Photographs by Kal Muller
Text by Jeremy Allan and Kal Muller

Designed by Leonard Lueras

First Edition 1988

TIMES EDITIONS

This page: A flock of migratory egrets over low hills in East Kalimantan.
Following pages: This liquid petroleum gas plant at Bontang and the oil refinery at Balikpapan, next doublespread, represent the national government's efforts to increase the value of precious natural resource exports. The oil processing business has made East Kalimantan among Indonesia's richest states.
The men who guide these shallow draft longboats through the foaming rapids of the Mahakam River and its tributaries must have keen eyes and iron nerves.
An orangutan skull substitutes for a human one in this updated Mamat ceremony, which the Kenyah Dayak perform as a rite of cleansing and purification.

Contents

East Kalimantan

Adventures in Borneo

Narrowing his eyes, his face set in single-minded concentration, Dani twisted both 40-horsepower engines to full throttle. A short run through smooth water helped build up speed, then his narrow 13-meter long plank canoe fought its way up through the rapids. Just past the last boulder-generated head of broiling foam, the Mahakam River funnels into a tight 20-meter stretch of surging water. With the consummate skill that comes from years of running raging rapids, Dani picked his spot. For several heart-stopping seconds, the craft made no forward progress even though both engines screamed full blast. In fact, the craft slipped, inch-by-inch into a slight backwards drift.

Pak Kerihon, the forward-lookout hunched in the bow, rocked his body back and forth in a vain attempt to get the boat moving forward again. Dani quickly glanced back over one shoulder to check on the boulders behind, then, nerves steady as those rocks, shifted his angle of attack slightly. The canoe began inching forward again, barely outmaneuvering the brute force of the river. When it began picking up speed, Dani eased the craft over to the bank to pick up his admiring group of foreign passengers. They included three men and two women who had met further downstream: an American photographer, an English dentist, a Singaporean woman and a French psychiatrist who was vacationing with a girlfriend. With a wide smile, Dani shyly responded to their numerous questions in Indonesian.

"That was easy, really. I've made it through far worse."

"How much worse?"

"Well, with the river two meters higher. Then there were eight big waves before the funnel. Today there were only three."

When the group arrived at the Raim Udang, the Shrimp Rapids, late the previous afternoon, there had been 17 waves; not even Dani could get through. He had managed to slide through the Haloq rapids, as his passengers held tight. But the drop in elevation had not been so drastic there. The scenery, however, was massively impressive; for more than a kilometer, the river was imprisoned by vertical, rock walls covered with vegetation and a curtain of thin, graceful waterfalls. Dani had made the passage look easy.

At the Udang, Dani advised his passen-

gers to walk around the rapids along a slippery path while he deftly maneuvered the canoe through. A warm, clear waterfall provided a cooling shower during the walk. One of the boatmen cooked up a pot of rice and noodles which tasted delicious for a change after the long, hard journey. Afterwards, the sound of the crickets and the rushing waters lulled everyone to sleep.

By the next morning, the river level had dropped four meters but the rapids were still fierce. The foreigners watched in awe while Dani nursed his longboat through the avalanche of water. Then they were all roaring upstream together again.

***The bountiful forest and river** provide for the daily needs of these Penihing Dayaks who show off their catch, two large river catfish **(left)**. Many of those Dayak who live in the hinterland remain skilled at hunting with a blowgun **(above)**.*

Further upstream, Dani shouted over the noise of the Johnsons. "Look ahead. Just there, beyond the next curve, you will see the waterfall."

And there it was, more than 30 meters high, pouring a thick, furious cascade into a side pool of the river. Dani slowed down so his passengers could get a good look, then pressed ahead, full throttle. He pushed the loaded craft through six more sets of rapids, taking a good-sized wave over the side once. Not even Dani is perfect, although the ladies in the group, casting surreptitious glances at his bulging muscles, seemed to think so. He apologized for the dunking and explained that the low water made the rapids even tougher. At those times, the Udang was child's play, for him anyway. In the early afternoon, the canoe reached the first uprapids village, Long Tuyok.

The men and women scrambled from the canoe up a notched log on the riverbank to a large wooden building, the longhouse, that formerly served as the communal living quarters for the village. Exquisite paintings of tribal motifs with prominent ornate dragon figures covered the posts in front. The longhouse now serves as a place for the ladies of the village to gossip while they pound rice for husking.

The main street of Long Tuyok was wide and paved with flat stones and flanked by homes on both sides. A few children followed them curiously, but no one pelted the visitors with the words "Hello Mister," that had become a tiresome Pavlovian refrain downstream. Adults politely acknowledged the strangers' greetings and went about their business. Men sorted and dried long strips of rotan, their principal source of cash income. Several elderly ladies whose earlobes were grotesquely distorted by dozens of heavy metal rings, walked by. It was a pleasant village.

But after a few minutes, the group was ready to proceed to Long Pahangai, a larger village a half-hour upstream. Long Pahangai is the gateway to a region of raw natural beauty and Dayak tribes that stubbornly cling to the old ways, an immensely exotic region deep in Kalimantan, as the island of Borneo is now called.

*The Erau Festival gives these young Dayak women (**right**) the chance to dance and display their finery before large crowds. Metallic sequins are now replacing the more intricate and delicate beadwork as decoration for Dayak festive clothing.*

Borneo. The name evokes images of brooding jungle and fierce headhunters, hazy memories of classic adventure movies about swashbuckling white rajahs in pith helmets, and even vaguer recollections of high school geography classes about a steaming, equatorial island, far from civilization, teeming with bizarre flora and fauna and warrior tribes who engaged in strange rituals. Remarkably, the reality of

has become an important oil and timber producer in modern times. Yet it remains a formidable frontier; pioneering Indonesians from all parts of the far-flung archipelago have ventured to the island to try carving their nation's future from its almost impenetrable forests. Petroleum refineries already gleam along the coast ringed by the sterile suburbs for their managers that seem to have been trans-

Kalimantan, as groups that travel up the Mahakam River discover, is not that far from those old impressions, even today.

Borneo is the world's third largest island, 750,000 square kilometers of primary rain forest, vast lowland and rugged mountains; East Kalimantan is one of four provinces that comprise Borneo's southern 70 per cent, a sparsely-inhabited corner of the Republic of Indonesia. Two provinces of East Malaysia, Sarawak and Sabah, and the tiny, independent Sultanate of Brunei, on the northern coast account for the balance of the island. Once the site of ancient trading kingdoms, East Kalimantan

Fishing with long hand-held nets in the rich coastal shallows provides a means of livelihood for those who live by Lake Jempang, an extremely shallow lake in the predominantly Islamic Kutai region of East Kalimantan (above).

ported whole from Sun Belt America.

This veneer of industrial progress and development vanishes quickly as you travel inland, however. East Kalimantan is one of the oldest settled regions of Indonesia and for two millenia or more, the Dayaks — a collective term for several distinct forest-dwelling peoples that have similar cultures — and the fishermen/farmers of the Mahakam Basin have remained largely untouched by the turbulent history of the East Indies. Instead, their lives have rolled along to the leisurely rhythms of river and forest.

Certainly the modern age is moving into East Kalimantan. But it's doing so with slow, hesitant steps. Some Dayaks use chainsaws to clear the forest for their neolithic slash-and-burn rice cultivation technique. In most of the traditional longhouses of the Dayaks, the rhythmic pounding of rice is accompanied by the equally-monotonous sound of a second-rate disco song booming from a cheap cassette player.

In recent years, most river dwellers have also purchased outboard motors for their wooden canoes. The new machine makes the daily trip into the quiet tributaries of the Mahakam easier. But when the men shut down their raucous engines in a quiet backwater, the centuries fall away; only the

ences to what may have been Borneo. After this brief mention the island disappears from Western written sources. Ethnographic data implies that the original inhabitants, the ancestors of the present-day Dayaks, were of Mongol genetic stock. These so-called proto-Malays are related to the Batak people of the island Sumatra and Torajans of neighboring Sulawesi, the island once known as Celebes.

myriad morning noises of the swamp forest accompany the setting of heart-shaped fish traps in the water.

Borneo has been an almost mythical area of unfathomable mystery and indescribable riches throughout history. Indian and Chinese ships plied the pirate-infested waters around Borneo for centuries, stopping at coastal settlements to pay fabulous prices for prized jungle products like camphor and bezoar stones, while the interior remained a trackless unknown. During the last century, independent European traders kept secret the location of gathering points on the rivers where Dayaks would bring their forest products for trade, enjoying a de facto monopoly until some competitor stumbled onto the location himself.

As early as the second century AD, the Greek geographer Ptolemy, made refer-

Latter-day Malays eventually established well-organized kingdoms at river estuaries and along the lower reaches of Borneo's three great waterways: the Mahakam River in East Kalimantan, the Barito in the neighboring province of South Kalimantan and the Kapuas in West Kalimantan. To the northwest, Brunei developed into the most powerful and splendid power-center on the island. In fact, the name of the entire island is believed to take its name from the pronunciation of the word Brunei which was corrupted by Western tongues.

The earliest-known Indonesian state, the powerful maritime Sriwijaya Empire based in South Sumatra, may have exerted some control over the west coast of Borneo and its diamond exports. But it was China's sporadic external trade and tribute policies that produced the first authentic, tantalizing glimpses of the island. Sixteenth century literature confirms the early trade relationships, indicating that Borneo's exports had reached India and China some centuries earlier.

Indian influence had a profound affect on Borneo during the early years of the Christian era. The first written record in all of Indonesia was found in one of the island's Malay kingdoms, Martapura. Kutai Martapura, as the local people called it, was ruled by a king named Mulawarman who ruled from what is now Muara Kaman on the lower Mahakam River. His reign is believed to have begun around 770 AD.

Like other kingdoms in Sumatra and Java, Kutai Martapura was heavily influenced by Hindu culture and religion. Sacrificial 'yupa' poles of stone, inscribed in the Indian Pallava script, attest to fourth

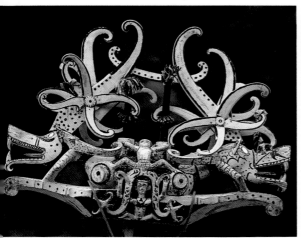

century rituals in which thousands of animals were slaughtered to win the gods' favor. These poles and rituals imply that the king was connected with India's Brahmin caste. Further inland, off the Telen River, a cave called Goa Khong Beng was discovered in 1895; inside, explorers found a dozen Hindu-style stone statues.

China's ties with the island started somewhat later than India's. It centered around trade of the "splendid and trifling" kind. By the 7th century, the China-Borneo connection was well-established. Whenever the island's current ruler thought it wise to ingratiate himself with Chinese power,

The tangled, swirling designs of Dayak carving reflect their forest environment, and their view of the world as living and interconnected (above). The weathering of the wood adds to the appeal of this hempatong, *or guardian spirit (right).*

tribute-bearing envoys from northwest Borneo traveled to China to kowtow before the Emperor. The Middle Kingdom's interest in the world of barbarians waxed and waned according to its internal problems and the emperors' divinely-inspired edicts and Borneo's expeditions of tribute reflected these Chinese vacillations: they continued punctually during Chinese expansionist phases, but were no longer considered necessary during the Celestial Empire's periodic introversions.

By the 14th century, winds of change began blowing towards Borneo. In 1365, Kutai Martapura rated but a passing mention in the Majapahit empire's famous *Negarakertagama* chronicle. Three years later, Javanese soldiers helped drive out Sulu marauders from Brunei.

The 16th century brought profound changes to Borneo: the introduction of Islam and the arrival of the first Europeans. Muslim traders from India successfully proselytized the kingdoms on Borneo's coast, as they did the coastal kingdoms of Sumatra and north Java. The societies of coastal Borneo were affected by the rise of Java's last powerful Hindu kingdom, Majapahit, which had wiped out several kingdoms, including one called Singosari. Refugees of Singosari sailed to the east coast of Borneo to fuse with Malays, who had long been settling around the Mahakam Delta. There, the Javanese refugees founded Kertanegara; the name probably originated from the last Singosari king who had ruled Java between 1268 and 1292 AD.

Rivalry soon developed between trade-oriented Kertanegara and the Mulawarman kingdom upstream. A royal marriage smoothed ruffled feathers for two centuries, but eventually the trading competition became too keen. This time, war resolved all problems: Mulawarman was defeated and its nobility wiped out.

Later, the Muslim faith began spreading inland into Dayak country, as a result of the proselytizing fervor of Kertanegara which embraced Islam in the first decade of the 17th century. At this time, the remaining seat of power on the Mahakam River became known simply as Kutai, from the Chinese "*Ko-Tai*" meaning foreign land.

The interior of a **kepala desa** *or* **kepala adat**, *is the everyday setting for this Modang family (**left**). Though longhouses still exist in the interior, increasing numbers of Dayaks are forsaking communal living for individual, Malay-style, houses.*

Portugal's Golden Age, which was characterized by an unrelenting search for spices and souls, produced the first European accounts of Borneo. Even before the conquest of Malacca, historical accounts in India proclaimed Borneo camphor eaten with betel as a medical wonder. Ludovico de Varthema, who travelled in Southeast Asia between 1503 and 1508, probably landed on the southeast coast of Borneo.

He wrote: "The people of this island are pagans and good people. Their color is more white than otherwise."

Though there was no immediate economic interest in Borneo, Varthema's description of Malacca as a major Eastern port perked up official Lusitanian ears. Within five years, Malacca was under Portugal's thumb and the feverish colonial races for control of the spice trade had begun.

The earliest verifiable firsthand description of Borneo flowed from the pen of a Spaniard, Antonio Pigafetta, chronicler of Magellan's epic world circumna-

vigation. Magellan himself was killed in the Philippines, but two ships in his expedition, the *Victoria* and the *Trinidad*, sailed to the Sultanate of Brunei in July, 1521.

Pigafetta was amazed to find a highly-developed civilization thriving on the island and a city of 25,000 families housed in wooden houses on tall pillars above the salt water. He was equally impressed by the royal treatment his party received:

" ... the king of that island sent a very beautiful *prahu* (longboat) to us, whose bow and stern were worked in gold. At the bow flew a white and blue banner surmounted with peacock feathers. Some men were playing musical instruments and drums ... When we reached the city, we remained about two hours in the *prahu* until the arrival of two elephants with silk trappings and twelve men each of whom carried a porcelain jar covered with silk in which to carry our presents. Thereupon we mounted the elephants while those twelve preceded us on foot with the present in the jars. In this way, we went to the house of the governor where we were given a supper of many kinds of food. During the night we slept on cotton mattresses, whose lining was of taffeta, and the sheets of Cambaia ..."

Life in the Lamin Mancong, a 350-year old long-house, recently restored and turned into a living museum. These views of the common area (above) and the front facade (above right) were taken before the recent extensive renovation.

Court etiquette did not allow the Spaniards to speak directly to the king. Their messages were transmitted through attendants attired in gold and silver, each sporting a dagger with a gold haft and adorned with pearls and precious gems. Here was the splendid Orient that the Europeans had dreamt about during their dreary, scorching, starving journey across the Pacific. According to Pigafetta's journals, the ban-

eventually won control over most of the islands that comprise modern Indonesia, including a large chunk of Borneo. They first appeared in the archipelago at the close of the 16th century when they were at war in Europe with Spain — and by extension with Portugal, which had been absorbed by the Hispanic crown between 1580 and 1640 — and had been frozen out of the lucrative Old World spice trade.

quet at the palace included "thirty or thirty-two different kinds of meat, besides fish" — all eaten with gold spoons.

After the news of the Spanish-sponsored world circumnavigation and conditions in Brunei drifted back to Malacca, the Portuguese in 1527 charted and began using the northern route to the Spice Islands, via Brunei. They preferred this longer but safer sea lane, even though Portuguese missionaries had begun to work in Banjarmasin on the south coast. Despite all the Portuguese activity on the periphery of Borneo, the east coast remained unknown territory, however. It wasn't until Pedro Berthelot's circumnavigation of the island in 1627 that the first fairly accurate map of Borneo's coastline was drawn.

Despite the earlier arrival of the Portuguese and Spanish, it was the Dutch who

Efficient, enterprising and ruthless, the Dutch set sail to obtain spices for themselves. In the process, they broke the Lusitanian monopoly and gained a toehold in the East Indies.

About the same time, English ships appeared in the area, asserting their right to a share of the trade. Most of the sporadic warfare occurred near the Moluccas, the world's only source of cloves, nutmeg, and mace until the late 18th century. Pepper was found primarily in Sumatra and Java. In 1635, Gerritt Thomasson Pool became the first European to visit Kutai and travel a short distance up the Mahakam. He also negotiated a worthless treaty with the Sultan. There were only two more recorded visits in the 17th century, but after the Celebes Wars, the power of the outside world would shake the somnolence of Kutai.

Historical Chronology

AD 2nd century — Greek geographer Ptolemy describes an island which could be Borneo. After this vague reference, there is no further mention of Borneo in western sources until Europeans begin exploring and colonizing the region.

4th century — The first written records of Indonesia, three stone *Yupa* poles with inscriptions from South India's Pallava Dynasty are erected at Muara Kaman on the Mahakam River by a shadowy but advanced civilization.

ca 770 — The Hindu kingdom of Martapura is founded at Muara Kaman, when the first king, Mulawarman, begins his reign.

ca 1280 — Settlers from Java, thought to be refugees from the defeated kingdom of Singosari, found Kertanegara at Kutai Lama near the mouth of the Mahakam. This new kingdom would soon come into constant conflict with the established kingdom of Martapura upstream.

1350 — Kertanegara and Martapura are temporarily united by a marriage between Prince Batara Agung Paduka Nira and Princess Indera Perawati.

1521 — Antonio Pigafetta, chronicler of Magellan's epic world circumnavigation writes the earliest verifiable first-hand description of Borneo.

1527 — Large-scale exploitation of the Spice Islands begin as the Portuguese navigate a northern route to the Moluccas, via Brunei. Although large numbers of European ships ply the East Indies waters, the Westerners would not turn their attention to East Kalimantan for another century.

1565 — Inhabitants of Kertanegara rapidly convert to Islam through the efforts of Tunggang Parangan and Ri Bandang, two Muslim preachers from Java.

Early 1600's — Kertanegara ruler Aji Pangeran Sinum Panji Mendapa defeats and annexes Martapura. His reign is marked by rapid expansion into Borneo's interior and the subjugation of Dayak groups, and outward beyond the coasts of Borneo with the annexation of several states in South Sulawesi.

1627 — Pedro Berthot circumnavigates the island of Borneo and produces the most accurate map of the island to date.

1635 — Five Dutch ships land in Kutai Lama. The Dutch sign a monopoly trade treaty with the Sultan, but do not return until 1671.

1699 — The kingdoms of Pasir, Kutai, Berau, and Bulongan were formally ceded to the Dutch. These territories now comprise the four regencies of modern East Kalimantan. Although these same territories were ceded to the British in 1812, and again to the Dutch in 1817, the local leaders remained firmly in control until the mid 19th century. As one observer noted: "The authority of the Netherlands government over Borneo did not extend past the coat of arms planted on the beach."

1701 — The first Bugis arrive in Kutai. These hardy seafarers and warriors from the neighboring island of Celebes, now known as Sulawesi, would play an important role in East Kalimantan history during the next two centuries.

1726 — Arung Singkang La Ma'dukeleng, a high-ranking noble of the Bugis royal family of Wajo in South Celebes, conquers the strongholds of Pasir and Kutai.

ca 1730 — Bugis settlers found Samarinda and soon become the predominant ethnic group on Borneo's east coast.

1782 — Aji Sultan Muhamad Muslihuddin founds Tenggarong, upriver from Samarinda, and shifts the court of his Kutai kingdom here.

1824 — Dutch Army Major Rehans Muller and his party are massacred by Dayaks acting on orders of the Sultan of Kutai, with whom Muller had just signed a treaty.

1826-7 — Bill Dalton, an English trader, spends 15 months in the Kutai area observing and writing about the inland Dayak population.

1844 — Erskine Murray leads a two-brig British task force to Kutai. Though initially well received by the sultan, fighting soon breaks out between the English and the sultan's forces, supported by their Bugis allies. One ship escaped but only after three Europeans, including Murray, lost their lives. Later that year, Sultan Muhammad Salehuddin formally recognized the authority of the Dutch Government over Kutai.

1846 — H. van Dewall is appointed Assistant Resident for the east coast of Borneo; he establishes his headquarters in Tenggarong.

1873 — Sultan Sulaiman and Dutch Resident Evaard Happe signed the "Lange contract", which gives the Dutch Government total economic control over East Kalimantan. In return, every Sultan received 105,000 guilden.

1879 — A Norwegian naturalist, Carl Bock, persuades the Sultan to accompany him far up the Mahakam, overland to the Barito watershed, and down the Barito to Banjarmasin.

1882 — The first coal mine is established near Loa Kulu and the first oil drilling concession is granted at Sanga Sanga.

1895 — The Sultan of Kutai abolishes slavery, but the practice continues for decades afterward in the inland regions.

1905 — Kutai is granted self-government, although the town of Samarinda remains under Dutch colonial control.

1919 — European observers report frequent head-hunting raids carried out by Dayak tribes. The Dayaks believed the head to be the source of power and magic — the skulls obtained would help them protect their village from all ills.

The Sultanate of Kutai was once a force to be reckoned within Kalimantan. Sultan Aji Muhammad Parikesit **(below)** gave up his formal power in 1960. His grandfather **(right)** was a charismatic figure.

1942 — The Japanese invade East Kalimantan. Although originally welcomed as liberators from the Dutch colonialists, their own harsh rule and uncompromising exploitation of Kalimantan's resources proves more oppressive for the local population than European colonialism.

1945 — The 1st Australian Corps land at Balikpapan in July, the last great seaborne operation of the war. The Australians stay until December, when they hand over authority to the returning Dutch. However, the Indonesians declare independence on August 17, 1945. During the next four years, the Dutch remain firmly in control as the Indonesian's struggle for independence is primarily played out on the island of Java.

1949 — The Dutch bow to the pressure of world opinion and acknowledge Indonesia's independence in December.

1950 — East Kalimantan is integrated into the Republic of Indonesia on April 10.

1956 — All Dutch-owned enterprises in Indonesia are expropriated.

1958 — Oil production rights are granted to PT Shell. But the production of petroleum becomes increasingly erratic during the next decade as Indonesia's political situation deteriorates.

1960 — The Sultanate of Kutai is officially abolished. Sultan Aji Muhammad Parikesit relinquishes all governing responsibilities and hands over his Tenggarong palace and much of his treasure to the people as a museum.

1965 — PT Shell is appropriated by the Indonesian Government which transforms it into a state-owned company first called PERMINA, and later PERTAMINA. During the next decade, the government encourages foreign oil companies to develop East Kalimantan's oil resources under a production-sharing contract system.

1978 — Rocketing oil prices bring unprecedented prosperity to East Kalimantan. Balikpapan, the seaport facing the Makassar Strait, mushrooms into a frenetic, over-crowded oil boom-town.

1983 — The largest forest fire in recorded history destroys 3.1 million hectares of primary and secondary forest. Though the fire is blamed on farmers who practice the slash-and-burn agriculture, the widespread destruction is fueled by logging debris covering natural firebreaks.

Although the Portuguese were the first Europeans to deal with the Banjarmasin Sultanate in southern Borneo, they met with little success; the independent Banjars sold only to the highest bidder. The Dutch also had problems. They signed monopoly contracts for pepper in 1635 and 1664; both were ignored by the locals. Only a permanent garrison could have enforced the monopoly, but at this point the expense was not worth the bother.

Holland's failure was due partially to Chinese competition. Not only did the oriental merchants buy pepper, diamonds and gold at better prices, they also snapped up high profit exotica such as camphor, tripang, shark's fins and bird's nests. At the turn of the 17th century, the English East India Company attempted to trade at Banjarmasin, but was quickly expelled by the

Dutch; the latter reasoned that if they could not enjoy a monopoly, no other European powers would.

Holland's perseverance in securing a spice trade monopoly had wide-ranging repercussions. After fighting their way to complete control in the Moluccas, the Dutch realized that much of the spice trade was then funneled through Makassar in South Celebes and eventually conquered it. Arung Singkang La Ma'dukelen, a high-ranking noble of the Bugis royal family of Wajo in South Celebes, conquered the strongholds of Pasir and Kutai in 1726. After declaring himself Sultan of Kutai, he

A shaman performs a ritual dance on the occasion of the secondary burial of a fellow villager (above). The bones of the deceased rest inside the coffin at left, topped with what is likely a carved ancestor figure. Other dancers also perform (left).

returned to his homeland to fight in local wars and lead an unsuccessful rebellion against the Dutch colonialists.

Around 1730, the Bugis founded a riverine trading town called Samarinda, now the capital of East Kalimantan. The Bugis' fighting and trading prowess, the rise of the Sulu Archipelago as a trading center, and the civil wars, all combined to remove the slightest remaining claims of Banjarmasin graceful freight schooners that ply the archipelago's monsoon-controlled seas. In the middle of the 17th century, the Dutch realized the Moluccan spice monopoly was being eroded away by Makassar-based Bugis traders. By exploiting local rivalries and flexing their military muscle, Holland forced Makassar to accept the Dutch as her sole trading partner.

The internecine fighting which Holland

over Kutai. Indeed, the whole east coast of Borneo moved into the Bugis orbit.

In 1782, Aji Sultan Muhamad Muslihuddin founded Tenggarong 20 kilometers up the Mahakam from Samarinda and moved the court of his Kutai kingdom there, reputedly at the insistence of the Bugis. By that time, East Borneo had seen the settlement of many ethnic Bugis from South Celebes; they excelled in naval warfare, were great shipbuilders — and still are. The sailors of South Celebes were great traders of the archipelago and the leaders of the most successful indigenous commercial operations, a tradition still maintain today by

The Naga is an important symbol of power throughout Southeast Asia, from Indochina to Kalimantan (above). The culmination of the Erau festival comes when the naga's head is removed, and the body allowed to float to the sea.

encouraged in South Celebes resulted in the loss of jobs among the nobility and a surplus of experienced soldiers. Many royal dynasties, like those of Kutai, and of Johore and Selangor in Malaysia, were either taken over by or united with Bugis and Wajo immigrants from Celebes.

In 1785 an army of 3000 Celebes warriors invaded the Banjarmasin Sultanate. The Dutch gleefully responded to a cry for help from the Sultan. With their superior weapons, the Europeans quickly routed the aggressors. As the price for this rescue operation, Holland installed a weak ruler on the Banjarmasin throne. The new Sultan soon acceded to Dutch pressure, yielding suzerainty of his own domain as well as the east coast of Borneo, over which he had only the most tenuous legal claim and practically no effective control.

During Europe's Napoleonic wars, England temporarily took over administration of the Dutch East Indies territories. At the time, only a limited number of territories were under Dutch dominion. But when Holland was allowed to return to her East Indies possessions in 1816, it realized that control over Java and a few strategic areas would not keep other European powers out of the archipelago.

Attempts to expand control were tentative at first, however. In 1825, Major Georges Muller had worked out a treaty with the Sultan of Kutai. When he ventured upriver, his party was completely wiped out by Dayaks acting on orders of the Sultan, who perhaps had had second thoughts about the treaty. Batavia did not however react to the killing.

Three years after the Muller massacre, an English trader named Bill Dalton ventured into the interior. Dalton spent 15 exciting months in the Kutai area, writing vivid accounts of the inland population of Dayaks. A series of articles in the *Singapore Chronicle* revealed an incomplete but tantalizing glimpse of the Dayak way of life: a war party returning with 700 heads, poisoned blowgun darts that kill in four minutes, and locally-forged blades cutting through musket barrels in one swoop.

On the commercial side, Dalton described Kutai's trade. The Dayak and Malay merchants brought down jungle products such as bird's nests — the most valuable export — along with beeswax, gutta percha, camphor and bezoar stones. Upstream traffic carried tobacco, salt, cloth, and pottery. Bugis and Chinese handled the overseas sector, where additional exports included *agar-agar* (a seaweed for traditional remedies), tripang (a type of sea cucumber), tortoise shell and gold dust.

Most of the trade went through Singapore, but was of no interest to Europeans. They considered East Borneo too far from the great trade routes. Dalton saw numerous commercial possibilities for his countrymen, however. His major mistake was to emphasize the ease with which Europeans could take over the area.

Meanwhile, the British began large scale trade with China during the Opium War of 1842. As a result, England acquired bases on Borneo's northwest coast. A bit further south of the British enclave, thousands of Hakka Chinese had swarmed inland during the modern era's first great gold rush in 1790. An estimated 200,000 finally settled in the region around Banjarmasin.

At that time, the island's mines were among the most productive in the world with yearly production of about 100,000 pounds of pure gold and the area quickly became Asia's main supplier. One source claims that West Borneo, for a time,

produced one-seventh of the total world output of the precious metal. The legendary Sir Thomas Stamford Raffles, who served as governor-general of the East Indies during Britain's five-year period of rule, wrote to the Governor of Bengal that "Borneo is not only one of the most fertile countries in the world, but one of the most productive in gold and diamonds." In fact, diamond mines in the Landak field in Borneo's south had produced enough valuable raw material to fuel the start of the Amsterdam gem-cutting tradition. By the 19th century, the mined-out diamond fields were abandoned.

Heads of captured enemies hold great magical power and protect the longhouse from disease and enemy attack. Orangutan heads in times past *(above)* were sometimes used in preference to human ones for curing and healing rituals.

Bookish on Borneo

Even before Hollywood began filming melodramatic movies in which adventurous soldiers-of-fortune explored islands like Borneo (Kalimantan) and encountered savage "Wild Men," writers had long been drawing cartoonish portraits of the island and its admittedly-bizarre cultures. Literature on Borneo abounds with sensationalist titles like With the Headhunters, My Life With the Headhunters, even I was a Headhunter (he wasn't). Most were written by publicity hounds in search of dubious fame and should be read only as pure escapist fantasy.

Better yet, you can kill time on those sweltering, tedious middays on a riverboat by reading one of the many well-written, accurate books about this fascinating island instead. Unfortunately for East Kalimantan, most focus on the former British colonies Sarawak and Sabah, which are states of East Malaysia, and Brunei, an independent country.

There is a wealth of wonderful reports and eyewitness accounts written by Dutch Colonials about their part of the island, but unfortunately most are gathering dust, untranslated, in the backrooms of university libraries and Asian studies institutes. Fortunately, there are many similarities between the Dayaks on either side of the Borneo border, in addition to some common elements of history.

For instance, Somerset Maugham explored the lives of British planters and civil servants in many of his short stories set in northern Borneo including The Outstation, but with a singular lack of understanding and even interest in the indigenous peoples. That

missing element, however, in itself reveals volumes about British attitudes toward the country's colonies.

Sir Alfred Russel Wallace, who developed the theory of evolution at almost the same time as Charles Darwin, tops the long list of naturalists who have made stylish contributions to literature about Borneo. His The Malay Archipelago, wordily subtitled The Land of the Orangutan and the Bird of Paradise, A Narrative of Travel with Studies of Man and Nature, has a hefty section on Borneo's flora, fauna and cultures; it remains a classic of literate naturalism.

Arguably, the best book on Borneo remains World Within, A Borneo Story, written in the 1950s by Tom Harrisson, a British special agent who went to Borneo during World War II and lived out his life in Sarawak to give the world one of the most comprehensive portraits of Borneo in his writings. Certainly no one has produced a more lively, entertaining yet profound ethnographic account than this book's first chapter on the Kelabit Dayaks. The rest of the book sparkles with true adventure as Harrison parachutes into Central Borneo and organizes native resistance to the Japanese.

In a more light-hearted, satiric vein is Redmond O'Hanlon's superbly-written Into the Heart of Borneo. It recounts the author's short trip into the island's interior with British poet/journalist James Fenton and their encounters with leeches, jungle rot, and the Dayaks. It is dryly humorous in the best English tradition. On the other hand, adventure almost leaps off the pages of James Barklay's A Stroll Through Borneo, an account of his five month walk through Sarawak and East Kalimantan in 1977.

An obscure grave a few kilometers downriver from Tanjung Redeb in Berau holds the remains of a Mr. Ohimeyer, a Dutchman who became the model for Joseph Conrad's first novel Almayer's Folly. Conrad wrote three other novels set in Borneo: An Outcast of the Islands, The Rescue and Lord Jim, and several short stories, including Freva of the Seven Isles and Karain. Although his total time in Borneo amounted to only a few weeks, all spent in Berau where his ship laid over for several days on its trading route, Conrad accurately portrays the tropical atmosphere and mystery and its affect on the sensibilities of foreigners at the turn of the century.

One of the earliest accounts of travel far into the interior of East Kalimantan is Carl Bock's The Headhunters of Borneo, published in 1879. Currently available in a handsome Oxford in Asia reprint edition, Bock describes his travels — in a somewhat overblown style — up the Mahakam, then down the Barito to Banjarmasin. Stylistic nitpicking aside, the book's merits rests on the author's early initiative to explore the unknown.

W ith one greedy eye cocked on potential gold profits and the other nervously set on the uncomfortable proximity of the British sphere, the Dutch finally decided to assert their control over East Borneo. In 1843 the Governor General in Batavia allowed further exploration and some administration in Borneo, but with much reluctance. Holland's manpower and financial resources were limited, with priority given to Java and Sumatra. The government reasoned that if a missionary or official were to be killed in Borneo, it would be necessary to outfit and send an expensive punitive expedition to re-instill the proper respect for whites.

Ironically, the official Dutch presence on the island began as a direct result of just such an attack, not on its own nationals, but on its British competition. During those chaotic years of empire-building, James Brooke, a young British adventurer who became the storied "White Rajah" of Sarawak, inspired many "men who would be kings". Brooke earned the title when he was installed as raja of Sarawak in 1841 after crushing a rebellion there. In an attempt to emulate Brooke, a Scot named Erskine Murray led a two-brig task force up the Mahakam in his bid to establish himself as a regional power. Initially well received by the Sultan, Murray's overbearing attitude soon alienated his hosts. On February 15, fighting broke out between the English and the Sultan's forces which were supported by their Bugis allies. The English ships managed to escape downriver, but Murray and two of his crewmen were killed in the battle.

News of the encounter reached Singapore, resulting in a garbled newspaper article giving the British side of the affair and Dutch bureaucracy creaked into action. A small naval force was dispatched to Kutai. The Sultan expected punishment and got off with only a scolding. Instead, he gladly accepted Dutch protection, an implication that no other European nationals were welcome in Kutai. In 1846, H. van Dewall was appointed as Dutch administrator for the Borneo east coast, with headquarters in Tenggarong.

*A **wary mother** and **scowling child** paddle their way to market in a Kutai village on Lake Jempang. (**right**). Living and working on the waters of river, estuary, sea and lake has long been a tradition for the peoples of insular Southeast Asia.*

traveling inland, Holland supported Christian proselytizing and moralized against head-hunting. Dutch officials even "punished" successful warriors with hard-labor prison terms apparently oblivious to the fact that the sentence was tantamount to a strenuous vacation to these seasoned jungle raiders; once the prison term was finished they received a hero's welcome upon returning to their longhouses.

permitted to enjoy coal and oil royalties which proved considerable after oil exploitation took off during the early 1900s. While Banjarmasin remained the principal town in Dutch Borneo through World War I, oil-boomtown Balikpapan took the lead during the 1920s. By then, according to one observer, "the great oil-producing center, with numerous and well-appointed tanks and modern equipment, reminded one of a

Wherever the Dutch found head trophies, the skulls were smashed and thrown into rivers. In the process the Dutch inadvertently prompted more head-hunting. They were unaware that most of those heads were old and retained little of the magic power that made them valuable to the Dayaks. The Dayaks quickly replaced the vanquished old heads with powerful new ones once the iconoclasts had gone.

Slavery was another practice frowned upon by the righteous Dutch, who ignored the fact that their colonial regime had imposed a form of slavery on the entire archipelago. The Sultan of Kutai abolished slavery in 1895, but the practice persisted for decades afterward in the inland regions. Although the Sultan's decree was purely symbolic, it again ingratiated him with his Dutch patrons. He and his heirs were

thriving town in America."

Meanwhile, the Dutch consolidated their hold on the East Indies and colonial administration made increasing inroads into the forests of East Kalimantan. Although the traditional Kutai lands along the Mahakam technically remained under the Sultan's sovereignty, the embryonic educational and medical facilities, and some crude infrastructure, marked the "civilizing" presence of the Dutch. To discourage the Dayaks from migrating from their longhouses to fill burgeoning employment opportunities on the coast, the administration subsidized food and fuel that went into the highlands.

Floating market stalls carry daily needs to river dwellers (left). Other intrepid businessmen offer simple meals and snacks to travelers (above), maneuvering their small craft up to river boats as they glide to their stops on the Mahakam.

Though East Kalimantan was being developed and organized, the ultimate benefactors of the colonial policies were the Dutch themselves. At best they were condescending; at worst they could often be harsh and uncompromising. The Dutch attitude toward their colonized territories won few hearts among the locals. When the Japanese juggernaut rolled through the Dutch territories of Borneo in 1942, the

Some months later, a party of Kenyah reported a strong force of Japanese two days downriver. For that the Dayaks, who were only trying to help, were locked up in four tiny cells. Three days later, the wives of the Europeans occupied these same cells. The Japanese executed all the men; they were either summarily shot, or, in the case of the Dutch Commander and Brooke Resident, blown apart by the opening

invaders were regarded — briefly — more as liberators than conquerors.

In East Borneo, the Japanese aimed for and speedily seized the essential oil-producing centers of Balikpapan and Tarakan. The Caucasians who did not surrender made their way inland to Long Nawang with unseeming haste. In peacetime this had been an important Dutch post, the only major administrative center located deep in the heart of Borneo. To the fleeing Europeans, Long Nawang offered the armed security of a regular Dutch camp. A large number of Dutch and English colonials, and some American missionaries, sought refuge there. They must have felt secure, but certainly underestimated the Japanese capacity for vigorous pursuit. The Japanese issued a surrender ultimatum, which was all but ignored.

Japanese mortar round that hit the veranda where they were playing bridge.

In East Kalimantan, the war ended with the landing of the 1st Australian Corps in Balikpapan, backed by a formidable sea and air fleet in the last great seaborne operation of the war. When the Australians left in December, 1945, Kalimantan was returned to the Dutch. But the Japanese occupation had boosted the confidence of the Indonesian nationalists in Java and throughout the archipelago. In December 1950, after a four year struggle for independence that was primarily played out in Java, the Dutch formally pulled out of their former colony. During the succeeding months, the three sultanates of Kutai, Berau, and Bulongan were incorporated into the nascent Republic of Indonesia, forming the province of East Kalimantan.

While the coastal regions embarked on their headlong, oil-fueled rush in the twentieth century, the inland regions carried on much as before. The Dayak societies lived in and off the forest the way they had for centuries; their contact with the outside world had been limited to a few Dutch administrators and the traders who traveled upriver to exchange salt, tobacco and other necessities for forest products.

erection of an important wood carving, and to complete the vicious circle, for support in warfare waged to obtain more heads. As money breeds money in the West, in Dayak culture skulls bred skulls.

To marry the daughter of a chief, no suitor need apply unless he could produce three or four freshly-severed heads as bride price for his prospective father-in-law. Impressionable young ladies in the West have

In the upland regions, the Dayak led a brutal life; there were endless rounds of warfare in which a male's prime concern was keeping his head and body in reasonable proximity. Traditionally, Dayaks believed that freshly-severed heads were essential for the spiritual and material welfare of the village. The supernatural powers of old skulls faded with age, however, and the search for new ones was a constant preoccupation.

The most powerful forms of magic power emanated from a newly-severed head, resulting in a vital transfusion of energy both to the village and to the individual who had obtained the prize. Aside from their spiritual power in controlling disease and harvests, skulls were needed for all great worldly events: the building of new longhouses, marriage and funeral rituals, the

a weakness for sports stars, but Dayak beauties on the other hand preferred young men who could back up their claims of bravery with gifts of head. One knowledgeable European wrote that the glamor of head-hunting victories even impelled some pretty young things to "break down the reserve that modesty normally imposes on them." Any head would do for spiritual purposes as well as for impressing the ladies. There was enough uncertainty in returning with one's own head still attached after a raid to really worry about the differences between the skull of a boy or a tough warrior.

The Makaham River is the link around which life in the Kutai region is organized *(left)*. A branch of the Mahakam runs through downtown Samarinda *(above)* in this aerial view. The river is East Kalimantan's main transport link.

A head-hunting raid was usually a well-organized affair with dozens or hundreds of warriors in the unit, led by a supreme commander. Although war parties could number as many as a thousand, the leaders usually preferred smaller groups to improve efficiency, logistics, and secrecy. Free-lance warriors had little chance of success on their own, although a single raider's prowess, alone or with one or two aggressive buddies, was highly-esteemed. But most commonly a longhouse community decided on a major raid, convinced one or more friendly villages to join, then elected a single, experienced war leader.

Each man supplied his personal fighting gear. The prime weapon was the *mandau*, a cross between a knife and cutlass. European travelers marveled at the skill of Dayak blacksmiths; working from native ores and primitive furnaces, they fashioned blades which held an edge capable of neatly slicing through a musket barrel. Some of the blades were artistic masterpieces, beautifully inlaid with copper, brass, silver, or gold, boasting exquisite filigree work. Handles were made of carved horn, with intricate, aesthetic patterns. The Kenyah and Kayan Dayaks sported the most handsome — and deadly — *mandau*. The instinct of self-preservation spawned elaborate defensive apparatus, anchored by a narrow body shield. The light wooden shields were carefully fashioned by following the longitudinal grain so that the enemy's *mandau* would become wedged, perhaps deeply enough to become stuck. In that happy circumstance, the warrior would throw down his shield and decapitate the disarmed enemy. Shields were bound with rattan to prevent splitting. The Kenyah decorated theirs with elaborate designs and tufts of hair from previous victims.

Other defensive items included a head-cap of rattan, rakishly sporting hornbill feathers if the owner had at least one skull to his credit. Body armor, also of rattan or kapok-stuffed bark cloth, and lucky beads or wooden charms completed the practical protection. A war coat of sun-bear or leopard skin added a touch of artistic magnificence to efficiency.

*A **Dayak woman pans for gold**. Though she can only hope to sift out a few grains of the precious metal **(right)** from the stream, more organized kinds of gold mining are now becoming a major industry in East Kalimantan.*

In the Land of the Dayaks

Much like the catch-all word Indian, the appellation "Dayak" encompasses a bewildering array of ethnic groups. The languages, artistic styles, customs and history of these people vary somewhat, but large and small-scale migrations within Borneo caused by population pressures, warfare and communications have blurred the differences, making it even more difficult for the marginally-interested colonial intruder or tourist to tell or distinguish between them.

In the most liberal use of the word, Dayak refers to any of the groups that live in Borneo's interior, as opposed to the Malays who have settled on the coasts and near the mouths of rivers; the Dayaks are mostly Christian or animists while the Malays on the other hand are Muslim. By that definition, some 400,000 of East Kalimantan's 1.5 million inhabitants could be classified as Dayaks.

Most travelers in East Kalimantan encounter one or more of the seven major Dayak groups living in the Mahakam River basin: the Tunjung, Benuaq, Bahau, Kenyah, Kayan, Modang and Punan. Most numerous are the Kenyah at about 40,000 who live in villages scattered along the middle and upper Mahakam and its major tributaries.

It was the aristocratic Kenyah who originated the distinctive art pattern of imaginative loops and baroque swirls that burst into a symphony of complex, colorful curves. But much of the monumental art work from the past has been lost, along with the traditional spirit worship that fueled its creation and gave it meaning. The Kenyah hail from the Apokayan, a vast region of rain forest to the northwest of the headwaters of the Kayan River deep in the interior. In the Apokayan, villages vary in size from 40 to 800 inhabitants. They lie along the upper reaches of the Kayan River, one of the major drainage systems of East Kalimantan, in Borneo's central highlands that slope up to the mountain range which delineates the border with the Malaysian state of Sarawak.

According to the Kenyah's oral traditions, their ancestors migrated to the Apokayan from the Belaga River area of Sarawak under pressure from wide-ranging Iban head-hunting raids. This shift occurred three generations before the arrival of the first Dutch official in the region in 1901. Scattered groups of Kayan already lived there; indeed, the name Apokayan means "Mountain Kayan," to differentiate this sub-group from Kayans living elsewhere.

After some small-scale warfare, the more numerous and better organized Kenyahs came to dominate the area. Both Kayan and Kenyah followed the usual customs associated with Dayaks: they built longhouses along rivers, warred and hunted with blowguns with poisoned darts, forged mandau swords

from local ores, and had a rice-based diet. Intermarriage between Kenyah and Kayan led to a large degree of cultural integration. Today, art forms and dances are so similar that only language distinguishes the two groups.

Everyone lives from shifting cultivation rice farming, supplemented by hunting and fishing. Social hierarchy remains important, although not nearly as much as it did before Indonesia became an independent nation.

Traditionally, society was ruled by an aristocracy; commoners and slaves comprised the majority of the population. Now marriages often take place between classes, especially since the disappearance of the mas kawin, the bride price which included old Chinese dragon jars, bronze gongs and rare beads. Nevertheless, members of the former aristocracy still command respect, tend to be village leaders and receive free labor for their rice fields.

In former times, the Apokayan was largely self-sufficient in all essentials except salt. There was trade in a few valuable, high-priced goods, like those used as bride prices, through one or more intermediaries. At least some of these items would be recovered with incoming bride prices as well as a by-product of successful head-hunting raids. Jungle products like bezoar stones from monkey or porcupine gall bladders, rhino horns and the highest quality camphor, all ingredients of exotic Chinese pharmaceuticals were exchanged for manufactured products. Salt was brought to the Apokayan from the coastal

regions or the Kelabit highlands in Sarawak.

The Kayan River tumbles out of Borneo's central mountains, crosses the highlands, then the rapids to the lowlands, then meanders to the town of Tanjung Selor before reaching the Makassar Strait. The rapids sever the Apokayan from river trade with the district capital of Tanjung Selor as well as Long Bia, the last upriver town where goods can be bought cheaply thanks to the navigability of the Kayan.

During the 1960's, the lack of communications and services led to a massive exodus. About 90 per cent of the Apokayan's Dayaks moved: 1,800 people from the area of Long Betaoh trekked for three days across the mountains to settle in Long Musang, Sarawak; more than 20,000, however, headed for the Mahakam basin. They built new villages for themselves on the main river or its tributaries. Popular resettlement areas included the vicinity of Tabang, Muara Wahau, and Long Bagun.

The migrations were led by the nobles and involved entire longhouses, sometimes up to 800 people at once. The routes and final settling places — in areas of scant or no existing population — were carefully scouted. Usually one year (and up to three years) was required to reach the new sites and people planted and harvested rice along the way.

For those remaining in the Apokayan, the situation began improving in the early 1970's when the people built several airstrips and skilled pilots of the Missionary Aviation Fellowship began flying into the isolated region. But the price of goods was prohibi-tive, as were passenger fares, to all but the wealthy and government officials. Only in 1986, with the completion of the longer airstrip at Long Ampung and government-subsidized weekly Merpati flights with Twin Otters, did the cost of passage and goods become affordable.

At present, two administrative districts cover the Apokayan: Kayan Ulu and Kayan Hilir. Due to the large scale migrations, the population of Kayan Ulu has dwindled during the past 20 years from well over 20,000 to 3000, all Kenyah, while Kayan Hilir retains only 800 people, mostly Kayan. About 75% of the region's population is Protestant, the rest Catholic. The beginnings of the Catholic missionary effort in 1967 coincided with the official end of the animist religion, although some praçtices remain.

The subsistence dry rice agriculture barely feeds the population of the Apokayan. In some years, the lack of rain or precipitation at the wrong time can ruin the rice crop. But there is no starvation: drought resistant tubers such as yams and cassava or sago from the jungle fill stomachs until the next rice crop.

The exodus from the Apokayan seems to have abated now; plenty of land is available and schools wide-spread, although short of teachers. Medicines and doctors are either in very short supply or nonexistent. Some government money is finding its way into the area — official wages and road, or footpath building. The subsidized weekly Merpati flights could become a decisive factor in stemming complete depopulation of the Apokayan.

51

Once the raiding party was organized, the local medicine man carefully scrutinized omens, especially the flight of certain birds. If the signs seemed favorable, the 30-meter war canoes quickly filled with eager men, eyes glinting. On a quiet stretch of water, muscular paddlers could spurt along at 20 kilometers an hour. Sitting two abreast, the two-meter wide, average-sized war canoe held as many as 70 raiders. An managed to approach without having been detected, they would stop on shore several hours walk from their target. Carefully hiding the canoes, they crept on foot the rest of the way, ensuring a path of retreat.

The ideal offensive strategy was to attack a longhouse at dawn, set fire to it, then pick off the defenders as they tried to escape either into the jungle or by canoe. Of course, conditions were seldom ideal and

occasional gargantuan craft, carved out of a single log, stretched over 45 meters. But the Dayaks usually shunned the largest canoes for offensive use because they were unwieldy to handle in rapids and hard to hide from the enemy's eye.

If the approaching party had been spotted by an alert member of the opposition, a group of defenders would try for a river ambush; as the war craft struggled through a nasty stretch of rapids, a tree that had been previously chopped through would be tipped onto the craft, crushing the enemy. Poisoned blowgun darts would then wreak havoc among the distraught paddlers fighting to get away in the swift, white water.

Some of the heaviest war boats sported a small brass cannon, but this was for defensive purposes; attackers always moved with stealth until the last moment. If the raiders the defenders were not sheep. At the first awareness of an attack, the air of the longhouse would become electric with aggressive defensive preparations. The men grabbed ever-ready heavy bars of ironwood sharpened at both ends and hurled them at the attackers, along with an assortment of other projectiles such as large rocks to smash wooden shields and super strength poisoned darts from blow guns. Sieges were uncommon. Within a few minutes there was either a successful counterattack — or the longhouse was aflame and the defenders were fleeing for their heads. Aside from head-on attacks to the longhouse,

Hornbill feathers, reserved for people of great status, adorn this Penihing man **(left)** *from the village of Long Apari. Dancers* **(above)** *wear chains of beads, bear claws and boar tusks while performing in the* **Erau Festival** *in Tenggarong.*

ambushing a group on their way to the rice fields was always another popular pastime. Left-handed raiders led these ambushes. Occasionally there were standup fights, one-on-one, between fully-armed and psyched-up warriors. Threats preceded the mortal combat. The exchange of compliments included polite inquiries as to the opponent's gender, then the genial vow to use his scrotum as a tobacco pouch. When the verbal foreplay ended, experience quickly determined the winner. Within minutes someone would lose his head.

Captive women and children enforced into slavery were a fringe benefit of a successful raid on a longhouse. The captured dwelling would also be looted of valuable heirlooms such as ancient beads, brass gongs, and, most prized of all, generations-old Chinese and Thai jars de-

corated with dragons. The entire village turned out and greeted warriors returning with heads and booty as heroes. The reception committee included attractive girls who put their modesty on temporary hold, and assorted ladies performing "wild and uncouth" dances with the heads, according to accounts of the time. As another bonus, successful warriors could preen themselves with hornbill feathers, wear jaguar teeth in their ears and submit to special tattoos, all designed to trigger unstinting admiration. The skulls, properly-treated after a ritual lasting several days, insured the village's prosperity for a while.

Hudoq dancers use elaborate masks, and represent spirits, many associated with the rice cycle. The purpose of these masked dances (right), common to various Dayak ethnic groups, is to attract the good spirits and repel the bad.

The bright colors of this beautiful caterpillar stand out among the greens and browns of the jungle (**below**). Orangutans (**right**) rarely if ever attack men, this one was surprised by a 19th century Dayak hunting party.

It's Got Some Wild Wildlife

Compared to veritable havens of wildlife like the sister Indonesian islands of Sumatra and, to some extent, Java, travelers expecting to find the Borneo's jungles teeming with animals are liable to be disappointed. Nevertheless, some of the world's most exotic species make their home in the island's vast rain forests. It's doubtful if any of the two-horned rhinoceros still roam East Kalimantan and there are only dubious sightings of herds of Asian elephants; wild boars, sun bears, deers and leopards are more prevalent. All in all, the Kutai National Park near Bontang has more than 60 species of mammals and at least 300 species of birds.

Among them is at least one international celebrity found exclusively in Borneo and Sumatra — the orangutan which in the Indonesian and Malay languages translates into "man of the forest." Indeed, it is an apt description of these large, tailless red-haired apes, a sadly-endangered species with a man-like character that makes it a prime candidate for anthropology's "missing link". Despite the humorous antics that have made it a beloved star of stage, screen and circus, orangutans are seldom seen in the wild and are remarkably shy around humans; villagers sometimes keep an orphaned orangutan as a pet until maturity.

Orangutans exist primarily on a diet of fruit and need a large area of forest to survive. The great bellowing calls sometimes heard in the forest are made by males, who are loners by nature, staking out their territories. Their rapidly-dwindling numbers has prompted the establishment of orangutan rehabi-

litation centers in Central Kalimantan. They also inhabit the Kutai National Park in East Kalimantan.

In addition to the orangutan, Borneo boasts numerous species of monkeys and apes, from macaques to gibbons. It's not uncommon to see entire families crossing a road in a timber camp. Because it boasts a conspicious nose like a burlesque comedian, the Proboscis monkey easily takes honors as Borneo's most ridiculous animal. It is exclusive to the island and has reddish brown fur, except for the arms, legs, tail, and ruff of the neck which are usually white. These large monkeys prefer the swamp forests and, traveling in large groups, are frequently seen along the smaller rivers of the Mahakam Basin. Only adult males sport this splendidly pendulous proboscis, which apparently enhances sex appeal and straightens out like a party whoopee whistle when they honk to ward off intruders.

Monkeys are not the only creatures that hang around in Borneo's trees. Colorful, tropical birds also thrive in them — and they are also popular with Borneo's huge snakes. Pythons measuring as long as 10 meters (30 feet) and weighing more than 135 kilograms (300 pounds) are the world's largest. They feed by suffocating their victims in their coils then swallowing them whole. On a more pleasant note, you're likely to hear the deep resonant hum and raucous 'g-ronk' of a hornbill in flight at least once a day in the jungle. To the Dayak, the hornbill symbolises the upperworld, and they believe these large, gawky birds have magic powers. The feathers and beak are used as symbols of heroism.

Other airborne creatures, not all necessarily birds, include flying foxes, not to be confused with the common fruit bat. Flying foxes, with wing spreads of up to 1.5 meters, are the largest variety of bat and have a distinctive head from which it takes its name.

Some interesting inhabitants also live in East Kalimantan's waters; the Irrawaddy Dolphin prefers the warm, muddy waters of Southeast Asia's great rivers. It is found in Burma's Irrawaddy, Vietnam's Mekong, and India's Ganges rivers as well as the Mahakam, only the grayish-brown back of this dolphin is visible as it breaks the water. Its favorite haunts are the vast, shallow lakes of the middle Mahakam basin.

Visitors to the forests of Kalimantan are not likely to be in the least bit disappointed by the numbers, variety — and immensity — of its rodents and insects. They range from beautiful, enormous colored butterflies and moths like Rajah Brooke's birdwing (named after its discoverer, Sarawak's White Rajah) to grotesque, giant winged beetles and cockroaches; to flying squirrels (which can't really fly; they glide like hang-gliders), to the dangerous, malarial mosquitoes, and the repulsive, leeches.

Almost as shocking as head-hunting to puritanical Westerners was communal living. Dayak longhouses sheltered anywhere from a dozen families to several hundred souls; these veritable villages on stilts could stretch more than a kilometer along the river fronts. Communal dwellings provided protection against attack.

Although they are rapidly vanishing from the banks of the Mahakam, long-

houses remain an excellent social lubricant, a physical framework for continual intra-group contact. While each family can retreat to a private bedroom, all other activities including cooking, socializing, craftwork, children's play, and discussions are concentrated on the wide porch running the length of the building. If fear of headhunters was the raison d'etre for the longhouse, the ideal of communal living and religion kept the longhouses thriving and united. Most rituals can only be performed in or close by the longhouse.

Traditionally, Dayak tribes were divided into three basic social classes: nobles, com-

This upriver Dayak girl is no longer required to wear lobe-stretching earrings, and has chosen to wear Western dress (above). In Kalimantan, all but the most recent migrants prefer to locate their villages on the river's edge (right).

moners, and slaves. In several of the groups, the nobles, who constituted 10 to 15 percent of the population, enjoyed prerogatives that included living in the central apartments of the longhouse. The social hierarchy was strongest among the Kenyah, who still accord labor and deference to the aristocracy. The nobles' daughters fetched the highest bride prices, the beads, pigs, and heirlooms which only other nobles could afford. Because these marriages involved invaluable heirlooms as eventual inheritance, all classes insisted on hard-working, head-slicing sons-in-law and post-marital fidelity.

Another vanishing Dayak tradition is the extensive tattooing of men and women, either as protection against disease or to permanently commemorate personal prowess. Some men spent as much as 600 hours under the painful needle while dammar and soot were tapped with a needle under the skin. Facial hair was considered unseemly and unmanly, so beards and even eyebrows were plucked.

Young girls had their ears pierced; as they grew older; they inserted large rings into the distended lobe until sometimes more a score of thin metal hoops, a pound of bangles, accentuated their beauty. Necklaces of beads — generally the older they were the more valuable — added status. Among the most prized were those called in some places 'lukit segala;' they were round, black with delicate white and orange markings, and the Dayak had a sharp eye for fakes. An account written 60 years ago mentions a necklace of Venetian beads belonging to the Sultan of Kutai as being worth 'an entire Dayak kingdom.'

All of these unusual body ornaments can still be seen among some Dayaks, especially the older generation, deep in East Kalimantan's interior today.

For the most part, though, Dayak lifestyle has undergone wrenching changes because of impact of Christianity, government, and the desire for several essential, and some not-so-essential, material goods. The essentials include salt, tobacco, metal tools and outboard motors, while the useless run the gamut from junk food to tacky cheap costume jewelery.

Education, too, has enabled some Dayaks to trade life in the jungle for jobs in air-conditioned offices or on offshore drilling platforms. One chief wryly describes the modern Dayak as "a young man in skin tight jeans and polyester shirt unbuttoned to the navel, brilliantined hair, and sunglasses lounging casually in the doorway of a Malay style house."

But even in these fast-changing times, many Dayaks still adhere to basic elements of the traditional way of life. Rice cultivation is the local mainstay, practiced using the primitive, environmentally-catastrophic

locating the crystals. No smoking was allowed during the search. When a camphor tree was spotted, the Punan cut a notch in the bark and smeared the sap on his fingers. Should he judge the sap to be similar to "juice from his own spear, he run back, kill wife. She has other mens. Is true." If the Punan does not see much similarity, he collects the camphor with peace of mind.

slash-and-burn technique. Communal labor in the clearing of the jungle and at harvest time continues to reinforce social bonds. While large, fun-loving groups of "tuba" fishermen who use vegetal poison to stun the fish are a thing of the past, net fishing remains important. The gathering of jungle products including rattan, fragrant "gaharu wood" bezoar stones, and camphor also continues to be a crucial activity.

Omens and rituals are still associated with certain jungle exotica, which is sold at absurd prices to Chinese and Arabs. The nomadic Punan are the cleverest searchers for valuable products, which they trade with remote Dayak villages for salt and tobacco. One recent account quoted a Dayak description of a Punan's search for camphor: "flights of birds were observed and dreams of girls insured success in

The silent, spear-tipped blowgun that looks like something right out of those old jungle movies, remains the principal weapon of Dayak hunters. Pigs, monkeys, and birds are the common prey, but Dayaks hunt anything that moves. Being mauled by bears and boars still make hunting risky, even for the skilled Dayaks. Patience and stoicism are the hunt's key ingredients: "In the jungle, nothing can be won unless the hunter can stand still for much of the day, regardless of fire ants walking over feet, leeches crawling up legs, biting flies buzzing behind, and mosquitos humming in both ears."

A household chore unchanged for centuries: a Dayak woman husks rice on the veranda (following page). Intricate beadwork (following right-hand-page) used for baby-carriers, head-bands and elaborate hats, is a Dayak specialty.

Of course, the intrepid traveler who endures the hardships of exploring the interior of East Kalimantan, far from the coast, will encounter his share of eye-opening age-old rituals and customs. In the perpetual darkness cast by the canopies of giant *meranti* trees, elements of ancient animistic religion remain quite strong, although even here the belief in spirits doesn't seem to preclude a few Christian warriors get their pick of the ladies, and need not labor in the fields for their rice. Alcoholic beverages are also theirs for the asking, with guarantees of no hangovers.

On March 30, 1980, the Indonesian government officially accepted the Dayak's traditional religion, Kaharingan. The Indonesian constitution recognizes the right to worship one god and the practice of five religions: Islam, Hinduism, Buddhism,

saints or modern conventions. Disease is still often treated by lady shaman who go into trances to exorcise the evil spirit; the technique can be used in conjunction with modern medicine. Pig's livers and the flights of birds are occasionally scrutinized for omens directing various activities.

A few Dayaks still believe that the place and conditions of life after death depend on the manner of one's demise. In a curious parallel with the Aztecs of Mexico, there is a specific heaven for the souls of those who drowned as well as the best of afterlives reserved for warriors killed in battle and women who died in childbirth. Deceased

The Dayak cherish the traditions of their ancestors, yet they are open to the influences of modern Indonesia, as seen in the dancer's lacey purple kebaya (above) and the Javanese batik worn around the neck of this head shaman (right).

Catholicism, and Protestantism. The reason given for the acceptance of Kaharingan, even though belief in indigenous spirits and elements of Chinese ancestor worship seem to dominate, was that it is an ancient form of Hinduism. Like Hindus, Dayaks hold harvest festivals in most communities. Harvest festivals are still widely-practiced; the rituals and dances celebrate and preserve the fertility and vitality of both the earth and women.

These ceremonies are seldom announced to the outside world. A lucky traveler who is at the right place in the months of March, April, or August still enjoys the delightful prospect of stumbling into an awesome display of traditional Dayak culture in all its primitive splendor. As an early traveler remarked: "Wonders never cease in Borneo."

Of Birds, Beads and Blowpipes

The striking motifs of Dayak decorative art and handicrafts reflect the swirling, looping patterns of Borneo's jungle world. Stylized renderings of birds and reptiles or simple geometric patterns adorn longhouses, religious artifacts and everyday objects alike, revealing the distinctive graphic sense of the Dayak people.

Woodcarvings rank among the most striking examples. Chiseled out of ironwood or bone with primitive implements, the coarse surfaces of Dayak statues, collectively called hampatong, enhance their primal, dynamic designs.

The largest of these figures are towering totems known as belawing poles; they contain a bizarre assortments of figures, human and otherwise, often with grotesquely protruding tongues and enormous phalluses which evil spirits reputedly find repulsive. Once these totems were used to guard longhouses and burial grounds; Dayaks believed they protected the village against disease and disaster.

Other tall wooden posts carved with tigers sitting on top of the heads of gruesome human-like creatures were used as sacrificial posts. Slaves and other victims were once tied to them then tortured to death. Today, the posts are used for buffalo sacrifices.

Smaller carvings known as karohei and penyang are richer in detail and reputed to possess curing properties. They come in human or animal form, both male and female, as well as a variety of misshapen oddities such as hermaphrodites and hybrids of humans and animals.

Although the Dayaks are rapidly losing their once

considerable metallurgical skills, blacksmiths still produce exquisite inlay work on the mandau, the traditional Dayak sword. These blades are about the size of a machete. The carved deer bone handles of the mandau and the arabesques that decorate the top of the blade add a sinister beauty to this deadly weapon. The sheathes are carved from wood with typical Dayak designs and feature a long pouch to accommodate a short sharp skinning knife.

The best-known armament used by the Dayaks, however (and by Hollywood movie-makers in every jungle epic filmed from the Amazon to the Congo) is the sumpit, or blowpipe. Each is carved at least two meters long from a single piece of ironwood; a sharp short piece of metal bound to the tip enables it to be used as a spear as well as a blowpipe. The tricky part is boring the cylindrical hole through which Dayaks spit bamboo darts tipped with poison from the Ipuh tree. Expert warriors and hunters are accurate up to 50 meters with the blowpipe; victims are said to die within five minutes.

The personal accessories and costumes of a Dayak are veritable works of art in themselves; thousands of tiny colored beads painstakingly sewn in detailed designs adorn many pieces of apparel. Tobacco pouches, headbands, baby-carrying baskets and men's caps are often decorated with yellow and black beads in intricate patterns. Necklaces of European-made glass beads traded for forest goods with Chinese merchants are a precious jewelry item.

Undoubtedly the most unusual canvas a Dayak uses to display his artistic talents is his own body. Tattooing, done by a brass needle struck with stick records heroic deeds, long journeys and other milestones in a man's life. Women also receive incredibly fine rank-related tattoos. But it too is a dying art; many of the younger generation frown upon the practice and tattoos are now seen mainly on elderly and middle-aged people.

Basketry is another Dayak specialty. Cylindrical woven-rattan baskets, decorated with geometric designs, last through years of hard daily use. Dayak weavings are generally brightly-colored since the advent of artificial dyes. The Benuaq Dayaks make a stiff fabric from woven palm leaves. Their famous bark shirt was inspired in the last century by the jackets of European traders.

Collectors have already depleted the villages of some of the best and most valuable examples of antique woodcarvings, beadwork, and basketry except for some of the most remote spots in the interior. The best old pieces now command high prices in antique shops in the region. For the bargain hunter, blowpipes are among the least expensive souvenirs. Try the itinerant vendors at most tourist areas in Java and Bali.

I t isn't even necessary to endure the long raft trip as far as Long Pahangai to sample some of the delights of Dayak culture. Long before reaching the difficult stretch of rapids that Dani helped get them past, his small group of foreign passengers discovered them just beyond Long Iram, a 36-hour trip from Samarinda aboard double-decker riverboats that carry passengers and freight. The group had met each other in Long Iram, then met the district chief, Sadik, who agreed to take them further upriver in his 10-meter long, wide-hulled longboat, for the price of the fuel. Only three hours ride beyond Long Iram, they arrived at Data Bilang, a Kenyah village with an enormous wooden meeting hall raised on stout stilts carved with human figures and topped by a wide band of interlocked swirling paintings. Ironwood

shingles covered the two-stage roof; each extremity of the upper roof ended in an upward sweeping of carved abstract curves, and curlicues and mythical hornbills and other figures were painted on the gables.

Nearby was a towering carved totem erected to mark a recent visit by President Suharto. Wooden warriors and other human figures in relief hung to the main shaft of the pole. The carving of a hornbill, the bird sacred to the Dayaks because of its association with the sky and life-spirits, topped the shaft and an ornate human face stared from under the hornbill. Beneath that, a dragon snaked downward.

Modern Kenyah carving follows the ancient motifs (above), with riotous swirls and arabesques, creating abstract designs. Guarding a modern longhouse, the human figure (far right) incorporates new elements like a wristwatch.

The group bathed in the river and spent the night at the village chief's house at his invitation. They awoke the next morning to the sound of brass gongs and a large drum that was calling the villagers to the meeting house for a ritual called a *Mamat*. It used to be performed as a greeting to headhunters returning from a successful mission carrying lots of trophies. That morning it was held in honor of the group of foreign visitors.

older men gathered around some sacred leaves, chanted and parted the foliage revealing a skull. The foreigners were advised in all seriousness, that it was not a real skull, just an anatomical model from the school. Of course.

The action then moved in a procession, accompanied by the gongs, out of the meeting house to a football field. Three pigs, suspended from bamboo poles,

At the hall, *Mamat* participants had already donned festive Dayak gear designed to honor the ancient spirits; the men's modern shorts had been concealed under traditional loincloths, leopard skin tops for the aristocracy, bead necklaces and a variety of ornaments protruding out of holes pierced in the ears. The guests were told that a leopard's tooth worn through the top tip of the ear meant that its wearer had chopped off someone's head a long time ago, of course, but the "of course" seemed somewhat less than emphatic.

The musicians beat the ancient gongs and long wooden drum in unison. Then the

Wielding rattan sticks and rattan shields, these Benuaq (above) fight a ritual battle called the Bahempas. *The wicker war is a sanctioned outlet for intervillage tensions, and is fought between champions from neighboring villages.*

squealed. The men gathered around the totem pole and made offerings of betel nuts and other items to the spirits. All chanted while some drew their parang, the local sword, in a spontaneous war dance. When the energy level reached fever pitch, the pigs were brought forward and the men slit their throats.

The *Mamat* then shifted to one side of the meeting house where the proceedings focused on a bamboo pole; its thin outer skin had been shaved back in curls and decorated with various branches. Women and girls joined the participants, gracefully dancing in a circle around the men. Several chickens were hauled out, briefly danced with, then lost their heads. The blood from the severed chicken head was dabbed on the knee of each man.

Back inside the meeting hall, the music

continued full blast. A fire had been lit in front of the skull and all the men gathered around to sing and dance with joyous, zestful leaps. Another pig was brought out and suffered the same fate as the others. Then a stately dance by a group of girls in costumes and beaded caps brought the tension level back to down to earth. The *Mamat* concluded with yet another war dance by men who looked fierce enough to

After the men got out of their hot *hudoq* outfits, the women danced atop a large brass gong, then performed a Sangkep. In the latter dance, two bamboo poles were held parallel to the ground and click-clacked quickly together as single dancers hopped in and out between them. Those whose ankles got caught elicited rounds of laughter. The show ended with two elderly men performing war dances. They danced

set out on a head-hunting expedition at a moment's notice.

Only a half-hour upstream in the village of Long Hubung, the group was treated to yet another ritual. This time Bahau Dayaks performed the *hudoq*, a dance in which large wooden masks with grotesque facial features are worn by men whose bodies are completely covered with stiff robes fashioned from strips of banana leaf. According to one interpretation, each of the eight types of *hudoq* mask represents a beneficial spirit and their collective in-tervention helps insure an abundant rice crop. The group later learned the super-natural beings came from a mysterious highlands region called Apo Lagan. The *hudoq* danced in a wide circle, then were joined by a long line of women making slow, stately movements.

separately in order to avoid actually coming to blows in the excitement. They grabbed shields and drew their parangs and set their faces in fierce scowls, then set out to slaughter imaginary enemies.

Back on the river the next day the visitors encountered canoes filled with spear-wielding men. They were told that the men were waiting to spear wild pigs as they swam across the Mahakam. In the village of Ujoh Bilang the group discovered that rain had swollen the river and Sadik would not be able to get them through the heavy rapids on his longboat. It was then that they met Pak Kerihon — and Dani.

Combatants wrap their hands in fiber and scarlet cloth to protect themselves during the Bahempas ritual duel (above). Though showmanship is an important element of this festival, passions can become heated, and blood drawn.

Plight of the Rain Forests

An airborne visitor observing the vast expanses of primary forest covering the land from horizon to horizon, or a ship's passenger watching the endless wall of luxuriant vegetation lining the shore, would naturally assume the land of Kalimantan to be incredibly fertile. Actually, unlike the volcanic soils of Java and Bali, the red clay of Kalimantan is among the poorest on earth.

The tropical rain forest is a hothouse of biological activity. But the constant, rapid cycle of birth and death, growth and decay is all played out in the top few centimeters of the forest floor. Dead plant matter barely begins to decompose before the nutrients are absorbed by the surrounding flora. Thus, few minerals find their way into the soil.

The vast rain forests of East Kalimantan contain hundreds of species of plants and trees from orchids to the carnivorous insect-eating pitcher plant which has provided so much inspiration for far-fetched science fiction stories. But far from being the dense jungle of underbrush of adventure films, the floor of these true primary forests is surprisingly uncluttered. Virtually all the sunlight is captured by the leafy canopy of the awesome dipterocarps 50 meters above, where most of the forest life takes place. These giant trees send out shallow roots to soak up nutrients from the top soil, while lianas, epiphytes and other parasitic plants entangle the trunks in a web of roots and vines.

Though portrayed as a riot of color and activity in fiction, or a brooding metaphor for darkness and evil in Joseph Conrad novels, the rain forest is actually a place of gloomy tranquility. It is sheltered from direct sunlight and strong wind like an enclosed vault or an unoccupied cathedral or palace. In the distance, a muted thump tells of a falling branch or tree, while a soft brushing heralds a primate swinging through the trees. A rain forest is one of the most fragile eco-systems on earth. If a single tree is cut down, a new sapling quickly grows in the gap through which sunlight enters, and in a few years the tree shoots up to close the canopy once again. But if a large stand of trees is cut down, as in a logging operation, the whole complex interlocking system collapses with it; secondary growth such as alang-alang, a useless sedge-grass, grows first, successfully competing against struggling new saplings, and rain washes away the few nutrients present in the soil. Before long, a once magnificent forest is transformed into a sprawling tangle of weeds and stunted bushes.

The Dayak and Kutai have lived in peaceful co-existence with the forest for centuries. In their shifting — or slash and burn — cultivation the farmers of East Kalimantan clear small plots of land,

reducing the plant cover to ash with controlled fires, and work the land for two or three seasons, planting alternate crops of rice, cassava, corn, and bananas. Then the farmer moves on to other lots, returning only after five to ten years, enough time to rejuvenate the soil and for the site to be reused.

This type of shifting cultivation can support a small population without destroying the forest. But population pressures and increasing encroachment on traditional lands by logging operations are forcing farmers to clear larger sections of primary forest and to re-work previously cleared sections before the land has had sufficient time to recover.

Logging operations cause the gravest damage. The larger, experienced companies practice a selective harvest system, in which only a small, controlled number of trees in each hectare are cut. But a large tree being felled will often pull down neighboring trees, and the heavy equipment needed to haul logs and clear roads not only destroys trees but it packs down the soil, causing serious flooding problems and inhibited plant growth.

Although, in theory, logging companies are compelled to reforest their concessions, large-scale tree planting began only in 1980. Even the companies most active in reforestation efforts have replanted only a small area of their concession lands. Most

companies, and of course illegal loggers, simply don't bother.

In 1982 and 1983, one of history's largest forest fires destroyed 20 percent of East Kalimantan's forest reserves, after an 18-month drought. Before it was doused by heavy rains in May 1983, the fire consumed 3.5 million hectares, an area the size of the Netherlands, with an estimated loss of about US$6 billion in timber. Smoke clouded the sky for weeks, occasionally closing airports as far away as Surabaya, 400 kilometers away on Java. Stands of timber burned like 60-meter high torches; according to one local environmentalist, "Several important species of trees and wildlife were wiped off the earth in a few weeks." The authorities placed the blame on Dayak tribes living along Telen and Marah rivers. A spark from a farmer's bush fire could have started the conflagration, but the Kalimantan rain forests had survived drought and fire in the past. This time, the forest's natural defenses had been weakened by intensive logging. Dried wood waste, clogged rivers, and large trampled areas of brush and scrub provided ideal fuel for propagating the flames.

As a result, Indonesia's parliament moved to strengthen environmental regulations governing its invaluable, irreplaceable rain forests; only time will tell if such moves prevent their demise.

Back of the Book

This section provides detailed information, invaluable tips and entertaining tidbits about East Kalimantan as well as the rest of the island of Borneo, now known as Kalimantan. The main maps depict East Kalimantan, its location on the island of Kalimantan or Borneo, and the island's location in the region. Little-known facts about the area are revealed in the Trivia section, including how the Iban improve their love-life by emulating the rhinoceros. There's also a section of suggestions to help you tour the region, including detailed maps of the Upper and Lower Mahakam River regions. Information and suggestions are given which allow you to explore areas where few, if any, tourists have ventured before. Best Bets is a digest of everything East Kalimantan has to offer, with tips on buying precious antiques and valuable forest products and advice on where to get the coldest beer in Borneo. Finally the Travel Notes summarize the essential basic information needed to get you to East Kalimantan and back.

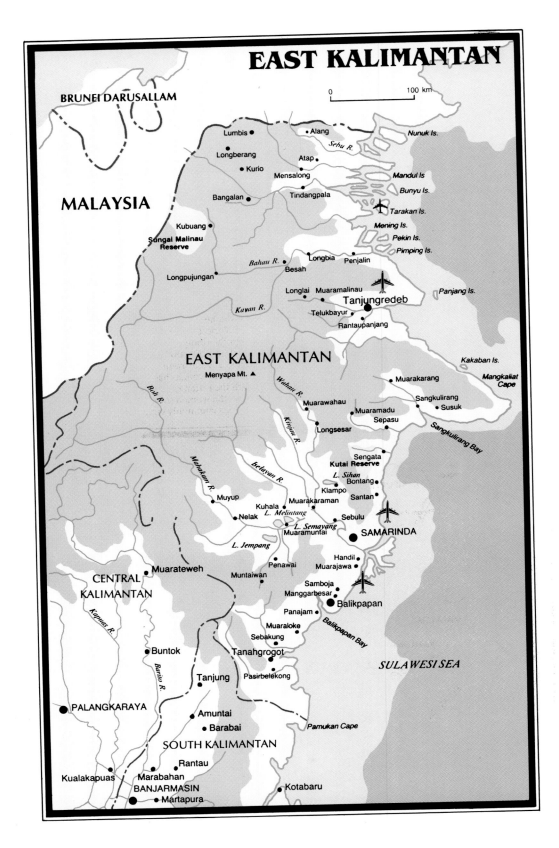

EAST KALIMANTAN

0   100 km

BRUNEI DARUSALLAM

MALAYSIA

Lumbis
Alang
Sebu R.
Longberang
Atap
Kurio
Mensalong
Nunuk Is.

Bangalan
Tindangpala
Mandul Is.
Bunyu Is.

Kubuang
Tarakan Is.
Sungai Malinau Reserve
Mening Is.
Pekin Is.
Pimping Is.

Bahau R.
Longbia
Penjalin
Besah
Longpujungan

Longlai
Muaramalinau
Tanjungredeb
Telukbayur
Kayan R.
Rantaupanjang
Panjang Is.

EAST KALIMANTAN

Kakaban Is.
Mangkaliat Cape

Menyapa Mt. ▲
Wahau R.
Muarakarang

Boh R.
Muarawahau
Sangkulirang
Susuk
Muaramadu
Sepasu
Kiniau R.
Longsesar
Sangkulirang Bay

Belayan R.
Sengata
Kutai Reserve
L. Sihan
Bontang
Muyup
Klampo
Mahakam R.
Kuhala
Muarakaraman
Santan
Nelak
L. Melintang
Sebulu
L. Semayang
Muaramuntai
SAMARINDA
L. Jempang

Handil
Penawai
Muarajawa
CENTRAL
KALIMANTAN
Muarateweh
Muntaiwan
Samboja
Manggarbesar
Kapuas R.
Panajam
Balikpapan
Muaraloke
Balikpapan Bay
Sebakung
Buntok
Tanahgrogot
SULAWESI SEA
Barito R.
Tanjung
Pasirbelekong

PALANGKARAYA
Amuntai
Barabai
Pamukan Cape

SOUTH KALIMANTAN

Rantau
Kualakapuas
Marabahan
BANJARMASIN
Kotabaru
Martapura

76

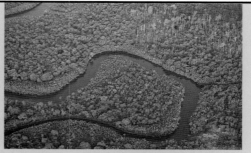

Trivia

THE NAME GAME. "Borneo" is believed to be derived from a corruption of the name "Brunei," the wealthy and historically important sultanate on the island's north coast. Kalimantan has two possible origins in Malay words: *Kali Intan*, or River of Diamonds, referring to diamonds found in South Kalimantan or *Kalamantan,* which is one of the many species of mango found in the area.

WANNA BUY A ONE-LEGGED DUCK? The Kutai fish for *gabus*, a type of catfish, in an extraordinary manner. They start with a live duck in one hand, and a fishing line with a piece of coconut on the hook in the other. When they hold the duck in the water, the duck's paddling attracts the fish. Just as a fish is about to bite, the fisherman lifts the duck from the water, and lowers the bait. The fish lunges for the bait, and is caught. Occasionally, the fisherman does not pull the duck away fast enough from the powerful jaws of the *gabus*; some say that accounts for the remarkable number of one-legged ducks in the Kutai region.

BET YOU HAVEN'T HEARD THIS ONE BEFORE. Local lore has it that a middle-aged, hirsute man in a remote Kayan village is the offspring of a union between a Dayak woman and an orangutan. According to his mother's story, she was a widow at the time, tending her rice field when an amorous orangutan kidnapped her. The ape kept her in his treetop nest for several days, where he consummated the strange relationship. In the meantime, she prepared to escape by collecting fronds of rattan while her captor was foraging for food. To bring her water, the ape would fill a bamboo tube and carry it back to the nest. One day, she poked a hole in the bottom of the bamboo pole. Thus it would empty out when the orangutan tried carrying it back to the nest, and he had return to the river for a refill. The ape made several round before he caught on. By that time, the woman had lowered herself from the nest with the rattan rope and escaped. According to the story, the woman soon gave birth to a hairy son. Such stories commonly circulate in many of Indone-

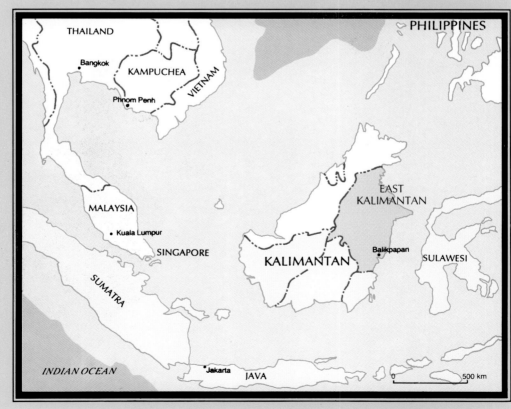

sia's lesser-developed regions and regularly enliven the columns of Jakarta's newspapers. However, most should be consumed with a grain of salt.

THE BUGIS. Indonesia's master seafarers, the Bugis people of neighboring South Sulawesi, formerly Celebes, have played a large role in the history of East Kalimantan. Centuries before the arrival of the first Europeans to the East Indies, the Bugis sailed from their home ports to the Spice Islands, to New Guinea in search of bird of paradise feathers, to Australia for tripang and to the great trade emporiums in Sumatra and Malacca. Famed as intrepid adventurers and traders, and feared as pirates, the Bugis alternately fought and allied themselves with the Kutai sultanates from the 16th century onwards, on several occasions helping Kutai win engagements with European ships. In the 20th century, large numbers of Bugis farmers have settled along the East Kalimantan coast.

A SULTAN'S TOYS. When the Sultan of Tenggarong wished to amuse himself, he would turn to his automobiles. Unfortunately, during the early 1900s Tenggarong's one navigable road was a narrow street about three-eighths of a mile — too narrow to permit turning a motor car around. For his joy rides the Sultan would order out all three of his cars, drive one down the full length of the short bumpy street, reverse gears, back up to the starting point and stop. He then repeated the maneuver with his other two vehicles.

DELIVERANCE. East Kalimantan's most spectacular stretch of white water, Giram Ambun — "rapids of spray" — is 33 kilometers (more than 20 miles) long. Even today, no one has successfully navigated a craft through the entire length of the foaming waters. In the 1930's, eight of the best Iban river pilots attempted a run. All of them drowned.

LETHAL WEAPON. A 15th-century Chinese annal reported that the Dayak "are skilled in throwing a circular knife, the edge of which is like a saw.' This weapon periodically surfaces today, accompanied by the proper sound effects, in kung fu films.

WARRIORS. Dayak soldiers distinguished themselves fighting against the Dutch during the Indonesian Revolution. However, most could not see the point of staying in the armed forces during peace time at that time, so no Dayak has been promoted to the rank of general in Indonesia's armed forces thus far.

CLIP JOB. The hugely distended earlobes of Dayak women are literally disappearing. The large metal rings worn by the women, which weigh up to a kilogram each, stretched their earlobes as far as their shoulders and, in extreme cases, to their breasts. Because the fashion is fading, however, even women who already have droopy ears are attempting to have them repaired. One upcountry doctor reports clipping 20 to 30 earlobes a week.

CULTURAL ECLECTICISM. Borneo's spectacular cultural eclecticism, a melange of centuries of disparate influence, is illustrated by an eyewitness account of a coronation at Brunei early this century. "The principal minister wore a turban and the haji outfit of a Mecca pilgrim; the two second-ranked ministers were dressed in Chinese and Hindu fashion; the fourth in a kind of loin cloth called 'Chawat' over his trousers represented the Bisaya warriors from the Sulu archipelago. Each minister declared the Sultan divinely appointed following ancient Brahmanic ways. The Muslim Imam then confirmed the Sultan as a descendant of Muhammad and Sri Turi Buana of Palembang (the center of Sriwijaya power in Sumatra) the founder of Singapore in 1160, whose line also became the royal family of Malacca."

SURE YOU CAN DRINK IT. Although the practice is not high on the recommended list of things you must do in East Kalimantan, you can drink the Mahakam River if necessary, at least if you take it from mid-stream. The lines of floating outhouses may seem a contributing factor, but the weak-tea coloring of the river stems from erosion — tons of soil are daily washed down the river from deforested land — and not entirely from the processions of outhouses and boats that float down the river. A half century ago, the Mahakam was clear.

EARLIEST ARCHAEOLOGICAL EVIDENCE. The oldest historic records in Indonesia were found in the lower Mahakam. Three stone *yupa* poles, inscribed in the Indian Pallava script, tell of third century rituals connecting the king with the Brahmin caste, and testifying to the slaughter of several thousand animals to win divine favor.

PALANG. One interesting personal accessory used by many Dayak males as a marital aid is the Palang, which is, well, let a Dayak describe it: "When you twenty-five, then you no good no more. Your wife she feeds up with you. Then you go down to the river very early in the mornings and sit in it until your spears is small. The tattoo man he comes and pushes a nail through your spear, round and round. And then you put a pin in there, a pin from the outboard motor." The "nail" is typically a rod of bamboo, wood or bone driven into the tip of the penis, further enhanced at each end with knobs or other vaginally-stimulating accouterments. The intrepid Tom Harrisson, the British World War II Special Operations Executive who settled in Sarawak and became a noted expert and author on Dayak culture, said the device was patterned on the penis of the all-but-extinct Borneo rhinoceros, which has similar naturally enhanced tip. In an item

in the Sarawak Museum Journal, Harrison hinted that he'd had the operation himself and confirmed that the palang was "in my experience decidedly successful" in enhancing the sexual pleasure of the women he tried it out on.

EXOTIC EXPORTS. Traditional exports from Borneo included well-known items like pepper, gold and diamonds. Aloeswood, also called *aquila* or eagles' wood, was the most expensive aromatic shipped to China. Today, some quantities of aloeswood is exported to the Arab world; its subtle, sweet fragrant smoke graces the traditional weddings and funerals of the wealthy. Benzoin resin, or gum benjamin, another aromatic export, was eagerly consumed by members of the elite who weren't quite so well-off. Until the 19th century, rattan was probably the most important of Borneo's exports to China, where immense quantities were turned into cordage. Today, much of the fine quality rattan dragged out of the island's interior forests becomes the handsome, light, furniture that can make any modern home look like a drawing room in a Somerset Maugham story. Other exports included:

• Bird's nests. The Chinese, who can make anything a delicacy, boil down the nests of the swallows found along the coasts of Borneo to extract the saliva used as a binding agent. When simmered, this saliva, which is mostly protein, is the prime ingredient in bird's nest soup;

• Gutta Percha, from the *jelitong* and other gum trees, which was used for medicine, adhesive, and as waterproofing for boats;

• Camphor, one of Borneo's enduring export. Crystalline scales of dried resin is extracted from the decayed heart of a *Drylobalanops Aromatica* tree. Camphor was used in the manufacture of traditional medicines and incense, and still used in some modern medicines;

• Bezoar Stones. A generic term for hard mucus deposits found in the alimentary canals of animals — chiefly ruminants. Borneo bezoar comes from several species of monkeys. These stones were an important ingredient in Chinese medicine;

• Damar, is the resin of the *Shorea* tree, used in perfumes and for varnish;

• Tripang, a tough sea cucumber. The Chinese tenderize it four hours to produce a tasty soup;

• Agar-Agar, white gelatinous flakes found in some seaweed, used in cooking;

• Hornbill ivory. One of the long list of Chinese aphrodisiacs, the "ivory" from the hornbill's prominent casque was a sought-after item.

THE TOWN BUILT ON OIL. East Kalimantan's biggest city, Balikpapan, was founded because of an oil strike, thrived and prospered on petroleum profits. Established in the late 1800s as the base for

BPM, the predecessor of Royal Dutch Shell, Balikpapan gained international prominence during the oil boom of the 1970s. Sepinggan airport became the country's second busiest after Jakarta's, and the poor and ambitious from all over the archipelago sought their fortunes in the ramshackle town located between the offshore oil platforms and the transplanted middle American suburbs on the hills.

The sprawling, Southern California-style company complexes remain a jarring contrast to the amiable disorder of the city below and seem unchanged from the boom years. But life is not the same. In the 70s, these complexes were filled primarily with expatriate executives and their families. Now through the process of Indonesianation, the replacement of foreign experts with qualified Indonesians, has changed Balikpapan from its previously stratified state. Because the pseudo-Spanish villas on Gunung Bakaran and Pasir Ridge are assigned by job position, increasing numbers of Indonesian middle manager are gaining entry to the chic complexes. Indonesian children ride brightly-colored bicycles along the well-paved roads, while a girls' football team, evenly mixed between Americans and Indonesians, practice on a large field.

Other sources of foreign revenue like timber, plantations, fish farming and gold prospecting offer some hope of replacing the lost oil income. But Samarinda, the provincial capital located on the Mahakam, is far better situated to exploit these resources.

Tours

Contrary to accepted wisdom, joining organized tours provide the better Kalimantan experience. The primary attraction of East Kalimantan is its traditional cultural forms, but an independent traveler is unlikely to witness Dayak dance and music unless he's lucky enough to stumble on a local event or wealthy enough to sponsor his own performances. Foreigners wandering through remote regions unable to communicate at least in Indonesian can be upsetting to the local inhabitants, who are disturbed at their inability to assist the strangers; hospitality is deeply ingrained in most Indonesian cultures.

However, independent travel is still possible, especially along the middle and lower Mahakam. A knowledge of basic Indonesian, or a good guide who can double as an interpreter, is highly recommended.

UP THE MAHAKAM The mighty **Mahakam River** dominates East Kalimantan; it is the region's life-stream and backbone, and a veritable super-highway with an extensive network of tributaries that reach to the remotest areas. The color of the water, usually a deep, brownish-yellow, often changes with the light as the river, sometimes several hundred meters wide, sweeps majestically inland in wide curves under a smooth, reflecting surface. Upriver and in the tributaries, swirls and eddies in the swift current discourage swimming very far from the banks. Crocodiles, once an ever-present danger, no longer cause problems. Most have been exterminated for their skins.

The Mahakam springs to life among the 1,500 to 2,000-meter-high Muller mountain range in central Borneo. It rushes downward for 100 kilometers, simultaneously accumulating volume and spouting off tributaries before reaching the first human settlement, the Dayak village of **Long Apari**. The upper Mahakam then flows past several dozen highland villages for about 50 kilometers before dropping below 150 meters above sea level by tumbling through a series of dangerous white water rapids which choke off all traffic, except for an occasional twin 40-horsepower driven canoe.

The Dayaks of the uprapids region live off subsistence slash-and-burn agriculture. Infusions of cash come from the export of birds' nests, rattan and some panned gold. A few outside traders and members of the local aristocracy control what little trade exists. High prices for essential goods such as salt, sugar, gasoline, soap and clothing result from the high transportation costs. The rapids have been known to overturn freight canoes with the loss of merchandise and occasionally even the expensive engines. Drowning is an occupational hazard of the boatmen. Between the rapids, a huge waterfall that

becomes truly tremendous after heavy rains spills directly into the Mahakam.

Long Bagun village, 300 kilometers from the river's source marks the upper limit of year-round, longboat-based communications and is usually the ultimate objective of foreign travelers who explore the Mahakam. From it, the Mahakam passes through 150 kilometers of valleys to **Long Iram**, a small river town that lies about half-way between the mountains and Samarinda. Long Iram is the terminus of scheduled, deeper-draft cargo-cum-freight riverboats, including twin-decked craft. Most of the year, these boats ply upstream as far as Long Bagun. But a dry spell in the inland mountains can quickly reduce the water level and prevent freight from passing Long Iram, which is located only 50 meters above sea level. **Samarinda** is the departure point for upriver travel. Lumber mills, coal depots, villages and houses built on stilts hug the banks of the Mahakam River. Floating platforms tied stationary to the banks often sprout a small, enclosed hut that serves as the residence toilet, as well as a spot for bathing and washing clothes. Sarong-wrapped ladies are seen nearby at all hours, busy with the family laundry. Everywhere, river-siders spend an inordinate amount of time brushing their teeth. This long leisurely process produces lots of foaming white mouths. No one seems the least bit concerned that the river water also serves as a huge toilet for all those living upstream. Foreign visitors on organized tours will be relieved to know that purified bottled or mineral water is provided for tooth-brushing. Those who set out on their own, however, will have to improvise.

Travel through East Kalimantan almost invariably means a journey on the turgid Mahakam, which entails boarding one of the many types of river craft. Generally, the further inland you go, the closer you get to traditional life, but travel also becomes more difficult, uncomfortable and unorganized. A good deal of moral fortitude is essential, along with a wry, fatalistic sense of humor and a highly flexible schedule.

When traveling aboard public passenger boats or cargo vessels, the difference between a relatively comfortable journey and a long ordeal hinges on remembering a few basics and understanding the Indonesian concepts of acceptable public behavior.

Ship etiquette calls for the removal of footwear on board, except on the hot tin roof which is the best spot for photography and tanning. Keep a pair of rubber sandals handy. Sneakers or bare feet are recommended in upriver areas where muddy banks and notched log ladders are often the only way to embark or disembark. Coordination and a sense of balance are also useful.

When first boarding, stake out your territory. That's easier if you board at the original point of departure and about two hours ahead of the estimated time of departure. There are several factors to look for as you select the spot you will occupy for the next few hours or days: the good spots for photography, the toilet, and the dining area, if there are any. Also remember that the boat can become uncomfortably hot during midday. Alternately, rain could be a problem. Stay away from broken windows, as sheets of water pour in unless the window is covered with tarpaulin. Most importantly, stay away from the engine and exhaust, which is smoky, hot, and noisy.

Passengers generally sit in rows on either side facing each other with luggage used as pillows or footrests. If possible, a space is left in the middle for movement. Everyone settles on an easily-cleaned linoleum floor. There is no problem while space is vacant and that is the best time to establish your ideal location. Spread out your luggage and lay down a woven leaf mat, which you can easily purchase prior to boarding. Other passengers will not move your luggage or step on your floor cover. You should also respect these taboos for other's floor spaces. But any empty linoleum is fair game.

As more passengers board, an empty piece of floorspace somehow miraculously expands from just enough space for a man's backside to sufficient room for his entire family -and their luggage. Try snapping a photo every ten seconds to document the process. The little bare space somehow takes over a bit of your territory as well as several others. A nudge here, a slide there and the deck cover's size is slightly reduced. Don't leave uncovered space near you, or you may find another family has moved in.

Of course, when things get really crowded, all notions of propriety are suspended. You might well end up trying to sleep with two pairs of feet in your face, while trying to keep your own extremities out of your neighbor's private parts. Forget any lascivious thoughts: you will never be sleeping next to an attractive member of the opposite sex unless you bring your own.

When nature calls, even the most fastidious Westerners are forced to go native. The facilities on riverboats consist of a hole in the floor of a structure hanging over the stern. Bring your own toilet paper, or follow the native way with your left hand and river water. Bigger boats have enclosed facilities, but the smaller upriver craft have only a board about 50 centimeters separating you from the curious stares of perhaps 30 children — and their parents. Foreigners are so different in every way, no doubt these gawkers expect them to do their duties through their belly-buttons.

As for the technique, simply observe how other passengers do it. Males usually pull off their pants, apparently river etiquette permits them to be seen in their briefs, then climb into the "john," squat down while pulling their underpants to mid-thigh level, then bend the head down between the knees, in a kind of ostrich technique. Women take a similar approach, wearing a sarong instead of briefs.

As for washing, simply squat next to the toilet in your underpants or sarong, and pour water over yourself from a bucket with a plastic pan. Stand up, soap yourself all over, then squat down again to rinse off with the pan. Then wrap a sarong or towel around your hips, pull off any wet undergarments and maneuver dry ones on before whisking off your cover. Men will find that shaving, like using the toilet, always attracts a curious audience, because the locals have little facial hair. Kids giggle as you grimace and scrape it off.

The lack of privacy can be a problem. You will probably be the only Westerner on a boat filled with people who have never had the opportunity to observe unpredictable animals like us at close range. Forget about fitting in. No matter what you do, you will soon learn that you are the proverbial sore thumb, free-of-charge entertainment, ready-made to enliven an otherwise boring journey for the local passengers. Extroverts will enjoy the attention; introverts will have to suffer in silence.

As for boredom, be prepared for plenty. Morning and afternoons are fine. There is a lot of riverside activity, pleasant temperatures, and good photography from topside. Not so during the hot midday hours which are fit only for the notorious mad dogs and Englishmen. At such times, a good book is indispensable. Try the tales of Joseph Conrad to keep you in the mood.

Virtually every craft on the Mahakam that does not have dining facilities has scheduled stops for meals from 6 to 9 in the mornings, 1 to 3 in the afternoon and 7 to 10 in the evenings. Near Samarinda, there's a surprising variety of cuisine, even succulent crayfish and, miraculously, cold beer.

Further upriver, be prepared for a heap of rice and a tiny piece of stringy chicken. Bring your own bottled water, hard boiled eggs, biscuits and anything else that will not mash together into a disgusting goo after two days in a plastic bag. You will be amazed at how good a can of Spam can taste after a week of tasteless rice in the interior.

You can either buy provisions in Samarinda stores, or pay somewhat higher prices to vendors who swarm aboard at downriver stops. But remember that they are your last chance. There are few vendors upriver.

Some four hours upstream, there's an obligatory stop at **Tenggarong** to report to River Traffic Control. Small boats laden with pots of steaming rice, fish, meat, soft drinks and more try to catch your craft as it drops speed and heads for the dock. These skilled peddlers can steer and propel their unstable canoes while vying for your attention. They will make a desperate grab for some part of your vessel, even while it's still moving fast, then hang on as it slides dockside, prepared to be the first to offer you a package of food wrapped in a banana leaf. Meanwhile, other vendors, carrying their wares in baskets, scramble aboard, often scurrying across the decks of docked river taxis. This is your last chance to buy most items. Ask a neighbor for advice on the correct price to pay; foreign faces can invite attempts at overcharging.

About four hours upstream from Tenggarong, your boat will coast up to a long row of floating food stalls at Senoni. Take your valuables with you, so you can relax while enjoying the jumbo crayfish and other tasty fare. Beer on ice is usually available. Prices are reasonable. Beyond Senoni, there are only occasional food stalls; you might have to climb up to a riverside village to look for a place to eat.

SHORT DAYAK CULTURAL TOUR This excursion can easily be accomplished in four to five days, requires a minimum of equipment and stamina, but provides a rewarding look at some of the traditions of Dayak culture.

It starts in Samarinda. Depending on the day, you can catch a riverboat directly to **Tanjung Isuy** or

take an express boat to **Muara Muntai**. Either way you will stop at **Tenggarong**, three hours upriver, for the inevitable assault by vendors where you can get some last minute provisions.

If there is no express to Muara Muntai on the day you wish to travel, you can alternatively travel as far as **Kota Bangun**, spend the night there, then charter a *ces*, one of the longboats powered by buzzing outboards that constantly ply the rivers. It's a half-day trip from Kota Bangun through Lakes **Semayang** and **Melintang** to Muara Muntai. The towns and villages you pass along the way are populated by Kutai people, descendants of the former subject of the sultanate. During the last three centuries, many Bugis from South Sulawesi have also settled in the area. The latest ware arrivals are Javanese.

From Muara Muntai, board a *ces* that will take you for the delightful two-hour trip through the 15,000-hectare **Lake Jempang** to Tanjung Isuy, where you can stay overnight in the Lamin (long house) Issuy, especially built to cater to tourists or a *penginapan*. The local *adat* chief will welcome you and, for larger groups, tribal dances may be performed. The next morning charter a motorcycle or walk the 14 kilometers to **Mancong**. Along the way, watch for bekantan monkeys, a cartoon-faced species with long red noses.

A key phrase in East Kalimantan these days is "channeled tourism." Authorities attempt to direct incoming visitors to certain specific areas, where they have a better chance of fully experiencing Dayak cultures.

While the serious traveler might frown upon such packaged cultural experiences, he might also spend weeks exploring the Mahakam River without ever seeing a longhouse or a *hudoq* dance.

The showcase for tourism development in East Kalimantan is the reconstruction of a 350-year-old longhouse at Mancong, the first phase of a U.S.$122,000 program to restore several abandoned longhouses in these Benuaq Dayak lands around Lake Jempang. Think of visiting a restored longhouse the same way you would visit the Borobudur, the enormous Buddhist stupa in Central Java that has also been given an ambitious facelift and structural refit in recent years complete with tidy, new landscaping.

The Mancong longhouse is an appropriate starting point; the 63-meter long, 11-meter high structure is a unique example of East imitating West imitating East. The *lamin*, as the longhouse structure is known locally, was originally built much like any other, with a single story and a storage loft. However, sixty years ago during a visit to Samarinda, the village chief saw a hotel modeled after a

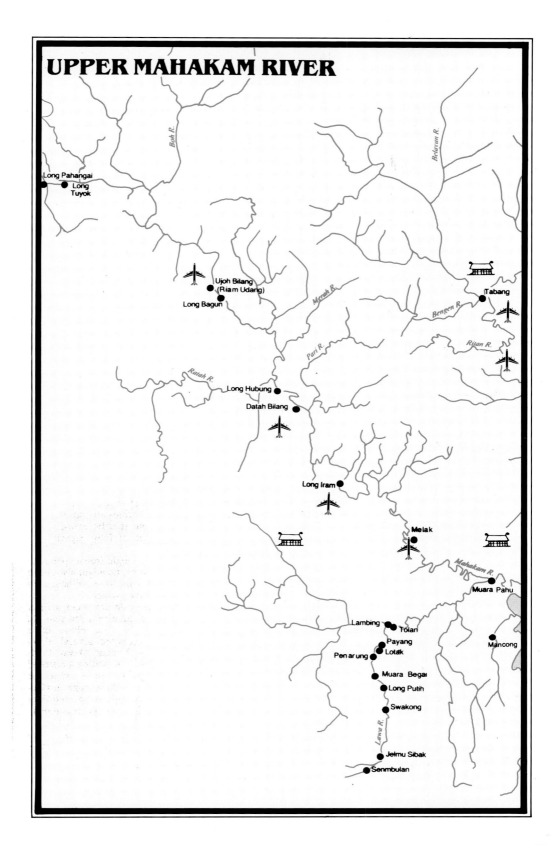

UPPER MAHAKAM RIVER

Long Pahangai
Long Tuyok

Ujoh Bilang
(Riam Udang)
Long Bagun

Boh R.

Merah R.

Belayan R.

Tabang

Bengen R.

Pari R.

Rijan R.

Ratah R.

Long Hubung
Datah Bilang

Long Iram

Melak

Mahakam R.

Muara Pahu

Mancong

Lambing
Tolan
Payang
Lotak
Penarung
Muara Begai
Long Putih
Swakong

Lawa R.

Jelmu Sibak
Senmbulan

83

longhouse, but with the addition of a second story. He was so enchanted with the overall concept design that he ordered a second level built onto his own long-house.

Unfortunately, the chief's attempt at architectural syncretism may have shortened the life of the original longhouse. In recent years the structure began leaning forward at a precariously steep angle. So the restoration team decided to completely demolish the original structure and rebuild it from scratch. Using only local materials, including a varnish made from tree bark, the team kept scrupulously to the original measurements, resulting in ceiling heights of distinctly Bornean proportions and beauty.

Oddly enough, because all but a few Benuaq Dayaks have lost their carving skills, most of the woodwork was performed by a carver named Karso from Jepara, the center of Javanese woodcarving. Karso faithfully reproduced the Benuaq motifs while acknowledging the centuries of mutual artistic influence of the neighboring Kutai societies by working their cultural motifs into his patterns.

The new longhouse has been developed as a "living museum," or eco-museum, by the government of East Kalimantan in cooperation with the Tropical Museum of the Netherlands. Local residents are encouraged to learn and practice traditional handicrafts in the longhouse, while tourists are invited to observe and make purchases. To keep the village atmosphere as traditional as possible, foreigners are not permitted to stay in Mancong overnight. You can stay for only a few hours, long enough to meet the craftsmen and enjoy a dance performance. Boats may be available to tour the villages upstream, where traditional Benuaq Dayak handicrafts are being redeveloped. You can arrange dances for $50 to $100.

Take your camping gear; you might be able to catch a ride on a *ces* through tranquil backwoods streams to **Muara Pahu**, where riverboats stop for meals in the late afternoon. Other points of interest that can be reached on motorcycle on ring road, include the 5,000-hectare **Kersik Luway Orchid Forest** in the Padang Luwai nature reserve, the **Old Lamin** of the Tunjung Dayak's **Sekolaq Darat**, and **Jantur Gemuruh** waterfall.

Catching any riverboat at Muara Pahu or Tanjung Isuy will get you to back to Tenggarong overnight. There you can top off your trip with a visit to **the former palace of the Sultan of Kutai**, Kertanegara. Turn-of-the-century travelers were impressed with the palace which showed off the Sultan's wealth and taste. According to one account of the time, "it was an immense building, erected upon a terrace overlooking the Mahakam, and situated about one thousand feet back from the river. It is constructed of wood, this being an earthquake country (sic), is painted a warm, light gray color, and has a broad-covered veranda extending entirely across the front. This covered porch is laid with polished planks of ironwood, glazy as tile and flinty as spar varnish. It has the natural polish which this wonderful wood takes. Not a nail was visible, the planks being doweled together and firmly secured in place by means of wooden pins, giving the entire floor area of 7,500 square feet the appearance of one piece of wood, so indistinguishable were the cracks between several planks."

The account gushed on: "The veranda opens directly into the great throne room, high-ceilinged, baronial hall with impressive proportions. Its dimensions being 60 by 120 feet. On the dias against the farther wall stood the throne of the Sultan and Sultana, and immense cut-glass chandeliers were suspended from the ceiling, while numerous tiger-skins covered the mosaic floor. . . The beautiful, multi-colored mosaic floor on which these royal tiger-skins were placed was laid by masters of the craft imported from Italy. At each end of the throne room there is a wide staircase with golden balustrade, and the steps are covered with scarlet Brussels carpet, its pile so long and thick I felt as if I were walking over a well-kept grass plot."

Unfortunately, the original palace, with most of its imported European furnishings, burned down in 1936. The present structure was designed by a Dutch architect. It houses the **Mulawarman Museum**, a repository for many historical Kutai treasures and Dayak artifacts. Also on the grounds is the **royal cemetery**.

From Tenggarong, it is an easy trip back to Samarinda or Balikpapan.

BEYOND LAKE JEMPANG Those able and willing to travel ten days or more will invariably want to venture further up the mighty Mahakam River and penetrate ever more traditional Dayak villages. You can explore the interior beyond Lake Jempang along several fascinating routes.

One alternative is to catch a boat from Muara Pahu south down the **Kedang tributary**. The riverbank here is overgrown with that climbing palms of rattan trees. There are scattering of villages of various Dayak ethnic groups.

Overnight in **Lambing**, the capital of the **Muara Lawa** sub-district. The next morning, you can set out on foot to the village of **Tolan** where there are two longhouses that were built by the Janulen, the chief tribe of the Benuaq Dayak.

Returning to Lambing, you can use the next day to explore the Muara Lawa sub branch river, a narrow passage of rapids and villages including

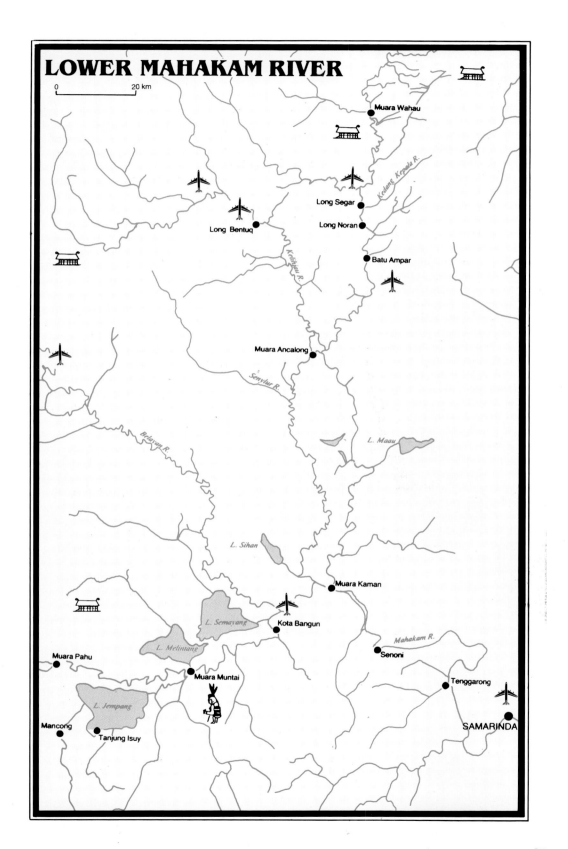

LOWER MAHAKAM RIVER

0   20 km

Muara Wahau

Kedang Kepala R.

Long Segar

Long Noran

Long Bentuq

Batu Ampar

Kelinjau R.

Muara Ancalong

Senylur R.

Belayan R.

L. Maau

L. Sihan

Muara Kaman

L. Semayang

Kota Bangun

Mahakam R.

L. Melintang

Senoni

Muara Pahu

Tenggarong

Muara Muntai

L. Jempang

Mancong

SAMARINDA

Tanjung Isuy

Rende Hempas, Payang Lotak, Muara Bagi, and Penarung. If it is ebb tide, however, you will have to walk instead. On foot, you can reach **Rende Hempas, Payang, Lotak, Titip, Long Putih, Swakong Jelmu, Sibak, Senmbulan** and **Sambung**.

The next day retrace your route back to Muara Pahu and Tenggarong.

LONG IRAM AND UPRAPIDS There is regular service to Long Iram from Samarinda, aboard the double-decker river boats, a journey of over 400 kilometers or at least three days. River taxis continue to **Long Bagun**, another 150 kilometers upriver. At that point, regular service is halted by rapids.

One alternative is to wait for a longboat carrying merchandise upriver. Because they are powered by twin 40-horsepower outboards these craft can burn up to 800 liters of gasoline during the run from Long Bangun to Long Pahangai.

Fuel is extremely expensive upriver and if you want to charter a craft, it is cheaper to bring your own drums of fuel from downriver. The most practical alternative, however, is to fly into the upriver airstrip at **Datah Dawai**, then wait — possibly weeks — for an inexpensive ride aboard any boat returning to Long Bangun.

The hassle of traveling here is rewarding, however. The Kenyah village of **Datah Bilang**, three hours beyond Long Iram, has an enormous meeting house with intricate carvings of human figures and the characteristic swirling motifs of the Dayaks are carved on the stilts and roof. A totem pole carved with wooden warriors and other human figures and

topped by the carving of a hornbill, the sacred bird of the Dayaks, towers nearby. It was erected in honor of a visit by Indonesia's President, Suharto.

A half-hour upstream is the Bahau Dayak village of **Long Hubung**. Here, dancers perform the exotic *hudoq* dance with its bizarre haystack-type costumes. Further on the river can get rough beyond the village of **Ujoh Bilang** at a spot known locally as **Riam Udang**, the Shrimp Rapids.

Those who successfully negotiate this stretch can dry out at the first uprapids village, **Long Tuyok**. Its most interesting feature is a large longhouse decorated with exquisite paintings of tribal motifs, and posts covered with ornate dragons.

A half-hour upstream is the village of **Long Pahangai**, the gateway to some of Borneo's rawest natural beauty and most traditional Dayak groups.
NORTH TO MUARA WAHAU Look for the slow water boat taxis bound for **Muara Wahau**. Rather than proceeding due west when they reach **Muara Kaman**, the first major stop on the Mahakam beyond Tenggarong, these craft will veer due north just beyond the town onto a major tributary called **Kedang Kepala**, about 120 kilometers from Samarinda. The name of this branch itself is enough to induce the truly adventurous to fancy themselves Lord Jim; Kedang Kepala means "Decapitated Head," a subtle reference to that most popular of Dayak pastimes in days gone by. You will spend your first night traveling up the Kedang Kepala, past the village of **Senyiur** to **Muara Ancalong**.

By the second night, you should reach the village of **Batu Ampar**, where you may tie up until morning, depending on river conditions. Just above **Batu Ampar**, the river narrows and the current swishes through, fast and turbulent and dangerous. Don't be alarmed if the driver guns the engine and hugs the bank; it's the only way he can make headway. From this point, it is fairly easy going to a point where there is a fork in the river. One branch, the **Kelinjau**, leads to the village of **Tanjung Manis**, inhabited by the Kenyah Dayak. Two hours further upriver, the Modang Dayak live at **Long Bentuq**.

By branching off to the **Telen River** instead, you arrive at **Long Noran**, home to another section of the Kenyah Dayaks. Here you will glimpse evidence of the Dayak world: a tall colorful totem planted in front of a meeting house. Long Noran is a recent village founded by Kenyahs who had lived several hundred kilometers to the north, around an isolated spot called **Long Nawang**. (Long means river in the various Dayak dialects.) Frequent food shortages and a desire to live closer to civilization prompted them into a mass migration. They left their ancestral homes. The first group of several hundred wandered for six years, planting crops and waiting for them to

ripen before moving to the next plot of land. They found their promised land in 1970 at Long Noran and nearby **Long Segar**.

More families followed the pioneers' jungle paths, looking for the good life: a place, to grow enough food, the essential salt for flavoring (prohibitively expensive at Long Bawan), medical facilities and schools.

This population shift has slowed to a dribble now that several thousand have resettled along the Telen River. Three years after several hundred families had chosen Long Noran as their new home, the Indonesian government legalized the move, helped to provide funds for clearing and housebuilding and started building schools and setting up health services. This is part of a general pattern in Kalimantan where the population from the interior is encouraged to shift to locations which are more accessible.

Beyond Long Noran, you will pass several lumber camps operated by a joint venture between Indonesian firms and America's Georgia Pacific company. By early evening of the third day, you will arrive at **Muara Wahau**, the region's administrative outpost. A courtesy call on the *camat*, or district officer, is mandatory, and often he will help you find a place to stay for the night. While most of the 400 inhabitants of Muara Wahau are Muslims, the 1,200 residents of the nearby village of **Slabing** are mainly Christians. The last settlement upriver, **Ben Hes**, can be reached during a three-hour ride by *ces*.

In most of these places, traditional dances can be arranged with a few days notice. Set a date before continuing upriver, then catch your scheduled performance on the way back. The cost is probably more than at Tanjung Isuy, but the performances are more authentic.

OUTSIDE THE MAHAKAM RIVER BASIN Few foreigners venture outside the Mahakam River basin. Those who wish to try can begin inland jaunts from any one of the larger coastal towns, or fly to **Long Ampung** on the upper Kayan River in the Apo Kayan region. Merpati Airlines has regular flights there. It also flies to **Datah Dawai** on the upper Mahakam, and **Long Bawang** in East Kalimantan's extreme northwest. Missionary Aviation Fellowship planes can also be chartered to any of the dozens of interior air strips but fares are expensive. Bear in mind that heavy rains can render any of the inland strips unusable for days, sometimes weeks.

NATIONAL PARKS VISITS There are two nature reserve areas in East Kalimantan. The **Padang Luwai** reserve between the Dayak villages of **Melak** and **Borong Tongkok** boasts 112 species of orchids — the black variety is unique. The **Kutai National Park** near **Bontang** features orangutans, proboscis monkeys, sun bears and a wide variety of birds.

Padang Luwai can be reached by taking a riverboat to Melak, a 24 to 36-hour trip by motorized longboat, or flying into its airstrip, then a jeep or motorcycle for the 16 kilometer hike into the park. As noted under the Short Mahakam Cultural Tour section, it can also be tacked on a side trip during a visit to Tanjung Isuy and Mancong.

Padang Luwai is an area of sandy heath land known as *kerangas* about 150 kilometers west of Samarinda up the Mahakam River. There are numerous kerangas areas in Kalimantan. They have an unusual drought-resistant or drought-adapted vegetation. (In this instance, drought refers to the instant leaching through the sandy soil of all rainfall, and with it most nutrients, rather than to any actual lack of rainfall.)

The Padang Luwai Reserve consists of three small plateaux: **Kersik Luwai, Kersik Serai** and **Kersik Kerbangan**. A forested valley separates the first two and Kersik Serai and Kersik Kerbangan are on either side of the **Nebeh River**. All three plateaux are dominated by two tree species, *Vaccinium bancanum* and *Tristania obovata*, both often found on the sea coasts as well. Ten species of epiphytic orchids also occur here. Wildlife consists mainly of some barking deer and mouse deer.

The **Kutai reserve** trip requires more time. A daily boat from **Samarinda** to **Bontang**, a five-hour trip, leaves the dock in front of the Central Post Office. Pelita also flies paying passengers for a fare of about $40 from Balikpapan on a space available basis. Several flights daily except Sunday. When the **Trans-Kalimantan Road** is extended to Bontang, mini-buses will do the trip in three house. Access to the southern and central parts of the reserve is also possible via the logging roads.

On arrival in Bontang, you must report to the **Nature Reserve Office** or PPA, on Jalan Mulawarman. The helpful staff, who speak some English, will arrange a schedule to fit your time and budget. The office will contact their field units by radio, advising them of your arrival.

The PPA has several guard posts in the field where you can sleep and purchase simple Indonesian food. Bring your own bedding. Basic costs are $2.50 per night for the accommodations; $1.50 for meals, and $5 a day for the guide (one is required for every three visitors). Boats run from $15 to $200 depending on size and speed.

The Kutai Reserve encompasses 200,000 hectares lying between sea level and an altitude of 340 meters. It is a rain forest of enormous hardwood trees. Wildlife includes sambar deer, banteng, bearded pig, barking deer, mouse deer, three species of leaf monkeys, and orangutan.

Best Bets

RIVERBOAT. The Al Muminun, leaving Samarinda every Monday for Long Iram, has individual berths with mattresses on the enclosed upper deck and a lockable storage space underneath. It also has two toilets. This boat generally offers the most interesting selection of fellow passengers as well, as it penetrates the interior of Borneo farther upstream than any other vessels.

WARUNG. The Ketemu Lagi in Muara Muntai is the place to kick back for a day. Gorge yourself on giant river prawns and suck up delicious coffee as you watch the river life passing by.

AIRLINE. Bouraq Indonesia Airways, Indonesia's third largest carrier, flies to home base Balikpapan daily from most points in Java and Eastern Indonesia. The leisurely pace of the Hawker-Siddeley propjets is amply compensated for by the attentive service and great view from oversized cabin windows. Bouraq also boasts the prettiest flight stewardesses and cheapest fares.

BREAKFAST. Bubur Ayam Samarinda on Jalan Antasari, Balikpapan (near the Hotel Benakutai), dishes up a huge bowl of rice porridge with chicken, just the thing for gray, damp mornings during the rainy season.

BEST BAR. The Tornado on Jalan Antasari has replaced the infamous Tit's Bar as the expatriate nightspot of choice.

BEST BUDGET HOTEL. The Hotel Andhika on Jalan Agus Salim in Samarinda, located near several good warung restaurants, has clean rooms, a friendly staff, and a sunny veranda from which you can observe the comings and goings from the mosque across the street.

TUAK. The people of Long Urog in the Apokayan brew the best palm wine; it's strong, somewhat tart, and guaranteed to numb your eyeballs after the third glass.

LOCAL DISH. The Haur Gading Restaurant on Jalan Sulawesi #4 in Samarinda features the best *Ikan Bakar*: cod or other fish grilled over open charcoal in the traditional Indonesian manner. This simple dish relies less on seasoning for exceptional flavor than absolute freshness of the fish and critically-controlled cooking time.

ART SHOPS. Souvenirs from Kaltim can often be cheaper in art shops than in the villages — if you can bargain. In Samarinda, try the shops along Jl. R.E. Martadinata, Jl. Awang Long or the Syachran Art Shop on Jalan Panglima Batur. In Tenggarong, go to the Karya Indah in Topsy and in Kutai the Karya Indah Art Shop. Prices in Balikpapan are higher but check out the Martapura on Jl. Letjen Soeprato and the Mustika Art Shop on Jl. S. Parman.

SULTAN'S PALACES. At the confluence of the Kelai and Segah rivers is the town of Tanjung Redeb. Just further up these rivers are the scenic Gunong Tabur and Sambaliung districts. In both areas the sultan's palaces have been recently renovated, and will be opened as museums very shortly. In Pasir, 4km from Pasir Belengkong, the palace also renovated, functioned as a local museum. Pasir Belengkong Sultanate was established in 1516 underr the name of Sadinangas Kingdom, and ruled by a queen named "Puteri Petung". Her spirit is believed to have been placed inside a bamboo or "petung" by Dewi Sri, Vishnu's wife.

PLANT. Kantong Semar, better known as the pitcher plant, has been the inspiration for such B-grade movie creatures the Triffids and Audrey II of "Little Shop of Horrors Fame." It looks like its name, having a yellow-spotted brown or green pod that attracts insects which finds the plant's "mouth" full of honey; of course, the unsuspecting insect then attempts to feed on the honey and falls through a veritable trap door instead. The mouth closes and digestive sap inside then allows this carnivorous plant to devour its prey.

WORLD'S LAST GREAT ADVENTURE. Anyone with a lot of time and money to spare can undertake crossing Borneo overland. You can charter a riverboat up the Kapuas from Pontianak to the headwaters, trek through the forest to the source of the Mahakam, then wait for a boat to Samarinda. For at least two weeks you will be in the deepest forests of Borneo, with only leeches and mosquitoes for company. Less intrepid, or more sensible, explorers can travel up the Barito River from Banjarmasin to the last villages, then trek for a few days to Long Iram, the terminus for riverboats.

AREAS TO MEET THE DAYAKS. The Bahu live in Long Ham, Long Bangun, Long Pahangai, and Muara Wahau/Slahbing. Kenyah, at the Kedang Kepala/Wahau branch of the Marah River, particularly in Tanjung Manis, Gemar Baru, and some villages along the Belayan River. Modang reside in Long Iram, Long Bagun, Long Pahangai, and Long Bentuk. Benuaq generally populate Barong Tongkok, Melak, Muara Pahu, Muara Lawa, Damai, Tanjung Isuy, Mancong and surrounding areas. Bentian live in Jelmu Sibak, Suakong Tuku, and Tente in the Muara Lawa district. Penihing inhabit the Long Apari district in the uppermost Mahakam river regions. Punan, one of Kalimantan's most isolated groups, are scattered around the Bulungan and Berau district and can also be found in the resettlement area at Ritan Baru.

MOST IMPRESSIVE DANCE SPECTACLES. The *Hudoq* of the Modang and Bahau tribe are worth the effort of searching it out. Also notable are the war dances of the Kenyah tribe and the knife and shield

dances performed by the Benuaq, Tanjung and Kutai to the tune of Dayak flutes and zithers.

REPTILES. East Kalimantan has the usual plethora of enormous pythons with reticulated jaws that are flexible enough to devour chicken whole and other snakes. But the honors in this category go to the tree-frog. It boasts long, fully-webbed toes which when expanded become larger than the body and permit the creature to glide from plant to plant.

FESTIVAL. An Erau, literally festival, that celebrates the founding of Tenggarong in September 1782 is held occasionally during that month. The last was in 1985. Attracting Dayak groups from all along the Mahakam, the festival is three days of dances, traditional sporting contests, reenactments of headhunting raids (simulated) and a final water fight aided by fireboats from Samarinda. This is one of the best opportunities to witness the color and spectacle of the traditional costumes, dance, and music of the Dayaks, without having to mount a major expedition to the interior.

THE SEA PARK OF PULAU KAKABAN. The County of Pulau Derawan comprises estuary and islands located in the Sulawesi Sea, including the islands of Derawan, Rabu-Rabu, Panjang, Semama, Sangalaki, Kakaban, Maratua, Bilang-Bilangan, Belambangan, Mataha and Sambit.

The Pulau Kakaban reefs are famous for the beauty of their coral and colorful fishes. It is also well known as Indonesia's biggest source of turtles eggs, producing almost 2.5 millions eggs a year. Also found are rare fauna like the Green Turtle (Chelonia mydas), the Scaled turtle (Eretmochelys imbricuta) and the Belimbing turtle (Dermochelys coriaceae). On the nearby island of Maratua can be found the rare trees Kayu Hitam and Kayu Cendana. Semama Island is a seabird sanctuary and nearby there is Panjang Island otherwise known as Snakes Island. On the island of Rabu-Rabu and Maratua one can find pearl diving spots and on the island of Kakaban there is a beautiful lake.

Pulau Derawan can be reached by longboat from Tanjung Redeb the capital of the district of Berau (± 4 hours) and from Tarakan (± 6 hours).

To go to Tanjung Redeb, you can fly a "Twin Otter" from Samarinda (1½ hours) or Tarakan (½ hour).

Travel Notes

Land and People

East Kalimantan is one of four provinces of the Republic of Indonesia that comprise the Indonesian portion of Borneo, which at 740,000 square kilometers is the third largest island in the world; only Greenland and New Guinea are bigger. The province straddles the equator (which bisects the island) and accounts for nearly a third of its entire area, 211,440 square kilometers of primary swamp, and mangrove forest, interspersed with cultivated areas. The Indonesian provinces of East, South, West and Central Kalimantan combined compose three-quarters of the island of Borneo. In the Indonesian language, East Kalimantan is known as *Kalimantan Timur*, or *Kaltim*, for short.

With more than 13,677 islands subdivided into a total of 27 provinces in all, most considerably smaller than Borneo, Indonesia is the world's largest archipelago; it measures 5,120 kilometers from west to east. Borneo is generally flatter than most of the nation's undulating volcanic islands. Half of the total land area of the Indonesian three-quarters of the island is under 150-meters elevation. Of Borneo's tallest peaks, however, many are located in East Kalimantan, including the 2,988-meter **Mt. Long Nawan** and 2,240-meter **Mt. Liangpran**. In contrast to most of Indonesia's other islands, there is no volcanic activity on Borneo, and earthquakes are rare and extremely mild. The absence of mineral-rich volcanic effluent has resulted in generally poor soil.

The island's second longest river, the 920-kilometer **Mahakam**, is located entirely within East Kalimantan and, inclusive of its tributaries, is the province's primary transportation network. Other long rivers include the 576-kilometer Kayan and 280-kilometer Sesayap, both in the northern part of the province. Most of Kalimantan's large lakes are also located in the province, including **Jempang** (15,000 hectares), **Semayang** (13,000 hectares), and **Melintang** (11,000 hectares).

Although the province of East Kalimantan alone is nearly one and a half times larger than the entire island of Java, Indonesia's nerve center to the south, this rugged jungle region has 1.5 million inhabitants, making it one of the world's most sparsely-populated areas; by contrast Java is one of the planet's most densely-populated islands, numbering more than 100 million people. Almost half the population of East Kalimantan is concentrated in the three coastal cities: Balikpapan, Samarinda and Tarakan, while the rest is scattered along the Mahakam River and in the hinterlands.

East Kalimantan is one of Indonesian's richest provinces, a direct result of oil and timber exploitation. Kalimantan's largest oil fields are in the Mahakam river valley and Tarakan Island. The large lucrative gas deposits in East Kalimantan's offshore territorial waters can be better exploited with the new advanced LNG plant in Bontang. Other exports include fish, cloves, copra and coal.

Getting There and Getting Around

By Air

Balikpapan has the second-busiest airport in Indonesia after the nation's capital, Jakarta. It's located in Sepinggan, just eight kilometers from the city. The airport at Samarinda has yet to be upgraded for large aircraft, so it's a long taxi or boat ride, or a short air-hop there from Sepinggan.

The national air carrier, **Garuda Indonesia**, has daily connections to and from Balikpapan to all major Indonesian cities. Garuda also flies to Balikpapan directly through Pontianak from Singapore, the small independent island nation west of Borneo, but most travelers enter Balikpapan via Jakarta.

Garuda Indonesia has an extensive international route network and many other major airlines also fly to Jakarta, most via Singapore, a 1 ½-hour flight away. Because of the oil business, Garuda offers four flights daily to Balikpapan, so fairly direct connections can be made, without having to stop over in Jakarta which is a lengthy 23-kilometer taxi ride east of the Soekarna-Hatta Airport.

Garuda also offers regular direct flights to Indonesia from the west coast of the United States via Hawaii, Guam, and Indonesia's easternmost international gateway, **Biak**, in the province of Irian Jaya. It is theoretically possible, although more complicated, to enter Indonesia through other international gateways like **Manado** in North Sulawesi on the neighboring island of Sulawesi to the east, and **Ambon**, in the Maluku island group.

Two other airlines, **Merpati Nusantara**, and **Bouraq Indonesia**, have daily turbo-prop service to neighboring islands at fares lower than those of Garuda. Bouraq has convenient connections to Samarinda for most of their flights into Balikpapan.

Merpati Nusantara serves the so-called *perintis* — pioneer — routes, flying passengers and cargo from Balikpapan and Samarinda into the hinterland. With the opening of these routes, journeys that once took days or weeks can now be covered in a 40 minute flight. Fifty-six airstrips are scattered throughout the interior, including Data Dawai on the upper Makakam, Long Ampung in the Apokayan, and Tanjung Selor, Tanjung Redeb and Tarakan on the coast. Several have weekly service. However, flights are often fully booked, especially on school and public holidays.

An alternative to Merpati is the **Mission Aviation Fellowship (MAF)** which operates two Cessna 185 aircraft from Samarinda. The five-seater planes are available for charter, including pre-arranged pickup at interior airstrips. Rates are in the US$200 range. The addresses and telephone numbers of the major airline offices in East Kalimantan are:

Garuda Indonesia. Jl. Pang. Antasari Balikpapan, Tel. 22300, or 21768.

Merpati Nusantara, Jl. A. Yani 2, Balikpapan, Tel. 22380 or 24452; and, Jl. Jendral Sudirman 57, Samarinda, Tel. 22624.

Bouraq Indonesia, Jl. Antasari 4, Balikpapan, Tel. 21107, or 21087; and, Jl. Mulawarman 12, Samarinda, Tel. 23011.

Mission Aviation Fellowship MAF, Jl. Ruhui Rahayu I, Samarinda, Tel. 23628.

By Land

A fully-paved, 115-kilometer road runs between Balikpapan and Samarinda and it has a 45-kilometer branch from **Loa Janan** to **Tenggarong**. The fare runs about the equivalent of a U.S. dollar. The road is being extended to **Bontang**. Another road, in varying degrees of repair, continues from Penajam, across Balikpapan Bay, to **Banjarmasin**, the capital of South Kalimantan. The trip takes 12 to 16 hours depending on bus breakdowns. Travel to some areas of the interior is possible using a 4-wheel drive vehicle.

By Bus

Buses and mini-buses leave more-or-less hourly from **Terminal** in Balikpapan and the **Samarinda Seberang Terminal**. The Balikpapan-Samarinda run, and vice-versa, takes less than two hours when dry, significantly longer during wet weather. In Samarinda, the public transport terminal is on the right bank of the Mahakam, while the city is on the left bank. Motorboats leaving from the pier at the central market, **Pasar Pagi**, connect the two. Fares are the equivalent of about $.25 per person, or $3. to charter the whole boat for your party.

By Taxi

Taxis from Balikpapan to Samarinda can be chartered in the Sepinggan airport Terminal (US$22) or in front of the Hotel Benakutai (US$23) or the Bus Terminal ($20). Shared taxis ($4) leave whenever the automobile is full. From Samarinda, the taxis leave from the Samarinda city terminal. The fare from Samarinda to Tenggarong is $12 for a chartered taxi.

By Sea

Indonesia has a national passenger carrier, **PELNI**, that provides the pleasant alternative of cruising through the country's islands, rather than flying over them. Four gargantuan, air-conditioned passenger ships, and two smaller ones, ply the archipelago's usually, placid, equatorial waters. The price of a comfortable first- or second-class cabin, equipped with private bathroom, color television, videos, and three meals a day is less than that of an air ticket between the same points. Other classes have correspondingly less luxuries, but provide an opportunity to get to know the gregarious Indonesians much better, partiucarly Ekonomi class where hundreds of families camp out in sleeping bags below deck.

The **KM. Kerinci** and **KM. Kambuna** alternate on the East Kalimantan route, providing weekly connections to **Balipapan** via **Surabaya** in East Java and **Ujung Pandang** in South Sulawesi, with further connections to **Pantaloan** and **Toli-Toli** in Sulawesi and back to the East Kalimantan port of Tarakan aboard the Kerinci. The Kambuna connects to Pantaloan and **Bitung** in North Sulawesi. From Bitung, cruise-lovers can catch the **KM. Umsini** for a trip on to **Maluku** and **Irian Jaya**.

For more information contact your travel agent or the following PELNI offices:

Headquarters, Jl. Angkasa 18, Jakarta, Tel. 416262, 417136, or 417319, Tlx. 44301, 44187, P.O. Box 115/Jkt.

Balikpapan, Jl. Pelabuhan, Tel. 22187.

Tarakan, Jln. Yos Sudarso, Tl. 202.

By River

Boats to upstream Mahakam leave from the old ferry terminal in **Sungai Kunjang**, just upstream from the bridge. Coming from Balikpapan, you can stop there to check the boat schedules before continuing to Samarinda by local taxi. To reach the terminal from Samarinda, charter a taxi from your hotel (approximately U.S. $3), or take a local taxi plying route A for the equivalent of about 30 cents.

Two single-deck express boats leave about 7 a.m. daily, traveling as far as **Kota Bangun**. An additional express boat leaves every day for **Muara Muntai**. One or two double-deck long-haul riverboats depart as well, heading far up the Mahakam or a tributary. Riverboats to each destination leave every two or three days. If you intend to board the larger craft for multi-night journeys, make sure you embark in Samarinda to ensure that you get a good berth.

Day trippers should embark at Tenggarong, where the boats stop about 10 am. Fares are $2 for the day trip to Kota Bangun, ranging up to $10 for the 36 hour journey to **Long Iram**. Ask a uniformed attendant at the pier for advice on the correct fare, because boat crews sometimes attempt to overcharge a foreigner. Pay when you disembark or shortly before.

Once upstream, *ces* — pronounced "chess" — also known as *ketingting* — pronounced like it sounds — is the primary mode of water transportation. These long canoey craft, powered by a noisy two-stroke gasoline engine, need only a few centimeters of water to keep moving. *Ces* can be chartered for $3-$5 per travel hour, depending on engine size. Bargain hard.

Customs and Entry Rules

All travelers to Indonesia must possess passports valid for at least six months from the day of arrival and a return or through air ticket. Nationals from 28 countries, including the United States, Australia, New Zealand and most non-communist European and Asian countries receive automatic tourist visa chops upon arrival that permit stays of up to two months in Indonesia, but extensions are not permitted. However entry by air or sea through ports other than Jakarta, Surabaya, Bali, Medan, Manado, Biak, Ambon, Batam and Pekanbaru requires a valid visa prior to arrival. Visas for a period of up to 30 days, extendable up to three months, can be obtained from any Indonesian Embassy overseas consulate.

Business visas must also be obtained overseas prior to arrival. A *surat jalan*, police permit, may be required for travel to some remote areas. Check with police headquarters in Balikpapan.

A maximum of two liters of alcoholic beverages, 200 cigarettes, 50 cigars or 100 grams of tobacco and a reasonable amount of perfume for personal use may be brought into Indonesia exempt from duty. Camera equipment, typewriters, radios and automobiles may be brought in, provided visitors leave with them, but they must be declared at Customs.

Pornography, television sets, radios, cassette recorders, printed matter in Chinese characters and Chinese medicines are prohibited. Penalties for bringing in narcotics are extremely severe and include the death penalty.

There is no restriction on the import or export of foreign currencies and travelers checks, but the import or export of more than Rp 50,000 is illegal.

The **head immigration office** in East Kalimantan is Samarinda, Jl. Mohammad Yamin, Tel. 23782. There's a local branch in Balikpapan at Jl. A. Yani, Tel. 21175.

Airport Information

An expressway connects **Soekarno-Hatta International Airport** with the Indonesian capital of Jakarta in Java, but allow at least 45 minutes for travel if you plan to stop over en route to East Kalimantan. There is an airport tax of Rp 9,000 for passengers departing the country on international flights and Rp 2,000 for all domestic flights.

Porters at Soekarno-Hatta should be tipped Rp 500 per bag (bear in mind that's less than U.S.$.50, so don't be stingy), and about Rp 500 at Balikpapan's airport in **Sepinggan.**

Other Essential Information and Insiders' Tips

Weather

Although East Kalimantan has no rigidly-defined rainy and dry seasons like most of the other Indonesian islands, the climate tends to be wetter from November to March. This can make travel easier, because the rains swells the tributaries and makes them easier to navigate. On the other hand, roads and footpaths deteriorate rapidly. February or March — just after the harvest — is the best time to see authentic Dayak dances and ceremonies.

What to Bring and Wear

Basic preparations for touring East Kalimantan involve more than packing the suntan oil and a bathing suit. Tour operators will provide all necessities, or inform you in advance of anything you must bring yourself. But anyone traveling further than the settled areas along the Mahakam in any way other than organized, packaged tours should take special precautions.

Clothing should include an Indiana Jones-style wide-brimmed hat, light windbreaker jacket, and rubber sandals, which are all available locally. Tennis shoes, the recommended footwear, are hard to find in western male foot sizes. Camel Adventure Gear boots and its ilk are okay for trekking through the rain forests, but not for boat wear or wading through rivers. For sleeping, a light cotton blanket and a small pillow are adequate for all areas but the chilly upriver highlands. All materials should be of lightweight cotton to help beat the heat.

Always pack a sturdy flashlight. Batteries are usually available, even in the most far-out reaches of Kalimantan.

The equatorial sun can be deceptively intense, even on cloudy days. Use the highest-powered sun screens on the market and tanning lotions at all times and always drink plenty of liquids. Overexposure and dehydration can be more devastating than some of the tropics' infamous exotic diseases.

Health

Valid international certificates for smallpox, cholera and yellow fever vaccinations are required for travelers entering Indonesia from infected areas, and will be checked at the airport. Typhoid, paratyphoid, and cholera vaccinations, though not required, are advisable, especially for tripping around islands like Borneo. Gammaglobulin shots will help reduce the impact of hepatitis, if not prevent it.

Your basic pharmaceutical travel kit should include water purification tablets, sunscreen, insect repellent, and medicine for small cuts, which will quickly become open sores in the humid forest.

Malaria pills are also a must, as the signs in many of the timber camps indicate. Popular brands, easily available from any *apotek* (pharmacy) in Indonesia, include Fansidar and Choloroquin. Although you can run the risk of liver or kidney damage by taking malaria pills weekly for several months or years, dosing yourself for a short-term stay should be no problem. Begin taking the pills three weeks before you arrive, and continue for two weeks after you leave the area. Wear long pants, long sleeved shirts and socks at night to lessen chances of infection — and to make it harder for leeches to get to you.

Bouts of diarrhea are common, not necessarily because of unhygienic conditions, but because of the drastic changes in climate and cuisine. The germs your body will encounter in Kalimantan are foreign to those it has developed defenses to in Cleveland. Newcomers should eat sparingly, but drink plenty of tea and other liquids. Chili peppers, a common part of the Indonesian diet, may actually help fend off some common stomach parasites, but may upset your gastric system if you're not used to them so go easy on the spicy food at first.

Raw vegetables can also cause stomach problems and should be avoided, unless you are eating in an international hotel, like the Benakutai.

It is unsafe, of course, to drink water directly from the Mahakam River with no noticeable side effects; foreign travelers should boil all drinking water for at least 10 minutes. A variety of refreshing bottled waters, many from mineral-rich Indonesian springs like Aqua, Vit and Oasis, are available in many provision shops, even far upriver.

Multi-vitamins — both for yourself and upriver villagers who will constantly ask for your help in treating a plethora of ills — are inexpensive in Indonesia. Cheap cigarettes and raw tobacco make good gifts for returning upriver hospitality. The Surgeon General's warnings haven't reached this part of the world, and if they did, it's unlikely they would be heeded. Aside from the usual toilet kit, a mirror, plastic soap dish, and your own cup are useful.

Hospitals

In the event of medical emergencies, Indonesia's best hospitals are located in Jakarta, or, if there is time to spare, catch the next direct flight to Singapore, which has international-standard facilities.

For heart attacks:

Intensive Coronary Care Unit (Cardiac Emergency) Central Hospital (Rumah Sakit Cipto), Jl. Diponegoro, 71, Menteng, Tel. 344-003

For burns and other emergencies:

Pertamina Hospital, Central Hospital/Pertamina Jln. Yos Sudarso Balikpapan.

Money

Indonesian currency is called *rupiah (Rp)*, not to be confused with India's *rupee*, and can be hard to handle. Even if you have a full complement of bills, they will always seem to be too small — or too large. The largest denomination is Rp10,000, but don't let all the zeroes throw you. That is the equivalent of less than U.S.$10. So for major transactions at banks and money changers, you may need to carry one tote bag just for the bills. Money-changers offer better rates than hotels and banks. When changing money make sure you ask for plenty of Rp1,000 and Rp500 notes, as peddlers, taxi drivers, and boatmen, and even provision shops routinely claim they do not have change for 10,000 or even 5,000 — even when they do.

In East Kalimantan, the government tourist department recommends money-changer **Haji La Tunrung** which has branches in Samarinda at Jalan Yos Sudarso, Nunukan and in Tarakan, also on Jalan Yos Sudarso.

Bargaining

Negotiating the price of merchandise is still a way of life almost everywhere in Indonesia, outside the fixed-price shops and boutiques of Jakarta. Approach bargaining as a friendly and enjoyable way of socializing with someone you might not otherwise have the chance to chat with and forget about whether you actually get a bargain or not. The basic formula is to offer half the asking price, then quit when you reach the maximum price you wish to pay for something. Often you will discover crafts and antiques are worth far more back home than you paid for them on a boat on the Mahakam.

Media

There are three English-language daily newspapers available throughout Indonesia: the *Jakarta Post, Indonesian Observer* and *Indonesian Times*. Large hotels and some book stalls also sell the *Asian Wall Street Journal, International Herald Tribune, Time* and *Newsweek*.

Language

Bahasa Indonesia is the national language, although more than 250 distinct languages and dialects are spoken throughout the archipelago, including Kalimantan where there are numerous Dayak languages. There are people who can converse in Bahasa Indonesia virtually everywhere in East Kalimantan, except the most remote regions. A compact basic

language guide available in some hotels and book-stores is *How to Master the Indonesian Language* by A.M. Almatsier. Some common Bahasa Indonesia words and phrases are as follows:

Bapak — used to address an older man or a male VIP.
Ibu — used to address an older woman or female VIP.
Nyonya — used to address a married woman.
Nona — used to address an unmarried woman.

Thank you	*Terimah kasih!*
Good morning.	*Selamat pagi.*
I want to go to . . .	*Saya mau pergi. . .*
the store	*ke toko*
the police station	*ke polisi*
immigration	*Imigrasi*
hospital	*rumah sakit*
What is the fare?	*Berapa?*
Stop!	*Berhenti,* or *Stop!*
Slow down!	*Pelan pelan!*
driver	*sopir*
ticket	*karcis*
taxi	*teksi*
airport	*airport*
north	*utara*
south	*selatan*
east	*timur*
west	*barat*
near	*dekat*
far	*jauh*
toilet	*kamar kecil*
I don't understand.	*Saya tidak mengerti.*
I want to buy . . .	*Saya mau beli. . .*
too expensive	*terlalu mahal*
Excuse me, or I'm sorry.	*Minta maaf.*
forbidden	*dilarang*
water	*air*
drink	*minuman*

Time
Kalimantan, along with Sulawesi and Nusa Teng-gara, runs on **Central Indonesia Standard Time**, which is GMT plus seven hours. There are two other time zones in the country: West Indonesia Standard Time, covering the islands of Sumatra, Java, Ma-dura is GMT plus seven hours; and, **East Indonesia Standard Time,** covering Maluku and Irian Jaya, is GMT plus nine hours.

Photography
Kodak and Fuji color films are widely available, but be sure to check the expiry date on the box to make sure it's still fairly fresh. Processing of Kodak Ektachrome slide film and color prints is good and there are numerous process shops in the big cities. Kodachrome is expensive, if available at all, and

includes the cost of processing which takes about amonth at the nearest Kodak plant in Australia.

For better natural light pictures avoid the intense daylight that occurs in the tropics from 10 a.m. until 3 p.m. A skylight will help reduce the bluish haze of the strong midday light. To compensate for the intense sunshine, try clicking down one f-stop.

Heat and humidity can ruin your film and camera. Carry and store your equipment with silica gel packets to reduce moisture. Be careful not to leave equipment in the sun.

Indonesian Customs and Taboos

The Indonesians are very polite people. Handshak-ing is customary for both men and women upon introduction or greeting, and smiling is a pleasantly contagious national characteristic. It is rude to point at other people with any finger. Use the thumb or gesture with the chin. To point using your toes is also considered offensive, particularly if you use your foot to point to objects on the ground. Indonesians rarely spank children but give them a stinging pinch instead. Light pinches are also given to children as a sign of pleasure. The left hand is never used to give or receive things, especially food or money. It is used for personal sanitary functions and traditionally considered unclean.

The vast majority of Indonesians are Muslims and do not eat pork. However, East Kalimantan has a large number of Christians and animists, and pork is often considered a delicacy in upriver villages.

Alcoholic beverages, except for some local brews like tuak, are also unpopular. During the fasting month of Ramadan, strict Muslims do not eat, drink or smoke from dawn until sunset.

Jam karet, literally "rubber time," means exactly what it says. meeting times can be extremely flexible so if you are a punctual person, be prepared to wait. There is an abiding concern about drafts and breezes, both natural or from electric fans and air-conditioning, out of fear of catching a cold or *masuk angin* (best translated as a kind of debilitat-ing flu.) Don't be surprised that the windows are kept closed on a sweltering hot bus, or on a passenger boat.

When addressing an older man, use the title *Pak*. With a mature woman, use *Ibu*. Address a young single lady as *Nona*. Avoid confrontations at all costs, in any situation, and always maintain your composure, even if the dry cleaners just mutilated your new silk dress. Strong shows of emotion must be avoided to maintain your self-respect. Stay calm and level-headed.

Accommodations
Because of the great influx of foreign experts, local

businessmen and fortune seekers during the oil boom years. Balikpapan and Samarinda have no shortage of accommodations. Hotels range from the multi-star luxury of the Hotel Benakutai in Balikpapan, to the comfortable rooms and great view offered by the Hotel Mesra in Samarinda, to clean, basic budget hotels in both towns. Upriver, however, the only option is booking into a *penginapan*, which is generally four walls, a bed, naked light bulb and a shared, cold water bathroom somewhere in the vicinity. The only exceptions are the Sri Bangun Lodge in Kota Bangun, under the management of Taman Raya Mahakam, which offers air-conditioning and hot showers, and the proposed tourist-standard bungalows in Tanjung Isuy.

Samarinda:
Mesra, Jl. Pahlawan 1, Tel. 21011
Lamin Indah, Jl. Bayangkara, Tel. 23836
Swarga Indah, Jl. Sudirman, Tel. 22066/76
Andhika, Jl. KH. Agus Salim, Tel. 22538
Hollyday Inn, Jl. Pelabuhan, Tel. 21185
Bone Indah, Jl. Ir. H. Juanda, Tel. 22240
Sukarni, Jl. Panglima Batur, Tel. 21134
Jakarta II, Jl. Dewi Sartika, Tel. 22895
Jakarta I, Jln. Sudirman Samarinda, Tel. 22624
Hidayah, Jln. Holid
Gelora, Jln. Niaga Selatan, Tel. 22024

Balikpapan:
Benakutai, Jl. P. Antasari, Tel. 21804
Miramar, Jl. Letjend Sutoyo, Tel. 22629
Blue Sky, Jl. Letjend Suprapto, Tel. 22267
Balikpapan, Jl. Garuda, Tel. 21490
Gajah Mada, Jl. Gajah Mada 100, Tel. 21046
Pirsa, Jln. Sepinggan, Bypass Balikpapan Tel. 21064 – 22981
Sederhana, Jln. Gajah Mada
Bahtera, Jln. Gajah Mada

Berau
Wisata, Jl. SA. Maulana
Kartika, Jl. P. Antasari
Tanjung, Jl Pasar baru
Herlina, Jln. Kartini, Tanjung Redeb

Kutai
Anda I, Jl. Diponegoro
Anda II, Jl. Tenggarong
Hikmah, Kota Bangun
Kutai Indah, Bontang
Sangkulirang, Sangkulirang
Sri Bangun, (Kota Bangun) lodge under Management Taman Raya Mahakam, Jalan P. Antasari, Balikpapan.
Hikmah, (Kota Bangun)

Bulungan
Nunukan, Jl. Nunukan
Sabar Menanti, Jl. Nunukan
Gracias, Tanjung Selor

Tarakan
Tarakan Plaza, Jl. Yos Sudarso, Tel. 21870
Bahtera, Jl. Sulawesi I, Tel. 21821
The Erly, Jl. Kalimantan, Tel 21185
Orchid, Jl. Jend. Sudirman, Tel. 21664
Barito, Jln. Sudirman, Tel. 21212
Mirama, Jln. Sudirman Tel. 21637
Sejahtera Jln. Karang Balik, Tel. 21472

Pasir
Ilham, Jl. Pasar pagi
Rindang Benua, Jl. Kartini
Gerogot Indah, Jln. P. Sentik, Tanah Gerogot

Tour Operators/Travel Agents

Samarinda
Pt. Duta Miramar, Jl. Jend. Sudirman 20, Tel. 23385
Pt. Masnun Anindya, Jl. Jend. Sudirman, Tel. 22624
Cisma Angkasa, Jln. Imam Bonjol 10, Tel. 21572-21392 Code telex 38147 VBS SMR.
Paradisa Indah, Jln. Diponegoro, Tel. 21598.
Angkasa Exspress, Jln. KH. Abul Hasan, Tel. 22098
Ayus Wisata, Jln. Agus Salim, Tel. 22026, Code telex 38177 AYUS I A

Balikpapan
Pt. Dhika Trabujaya, Jl. Gn. Sari Ilir, Tel. 22483
Pt. candra Wirapati, Jl. P. Antasari, Tel. 21663
Tomaco
Jln. P. Antasai, Tel. 21747, Code telex 45238 TOMA I A

Tarakan
Pt. Angkasa Express, Jl. Sebengkok, Tel. 21130
Pt. Sumbu Nusantara, Jl. Jend. Sudirman, Tel. 21656

Government Tourist Information Offices
Kanwil Depparpostel XIII Kalimantan Timur Jl. Jenderal Sudirman No. 33, Tel. 22286 Samarinda.
Dinas Pariwisata Propinsi Daerah Tk. I Kalimantan Timur
(East Kalimantan Regional Tourism Service) Jl. Ade Irma Suryani No. 1, Tel. 21669 Samarinda.

Festivals and Holidays

Many of the holidays in Indonesia are Muslim religious observances, but as a reflection of Pancasila, the state philosophy, Christian, Buddhist and Hindu holidays are also observed. The dates of the Muslim holidays vary, usually occurring about ten days earlier with each successive year.

Index

Back of Book: Photo Captions

(p. 77)   *The river Mahakam swirling through the jungle*

(p. 78)   *Floating market stall*

(p. 79)   *Traditional means of cultivation*

(p. 80)   *A village along the river Mahakam*

(p. 81, left)   *Manufacturing of a parang (sword)*

(p. 81, right)   *Carving a hampatong*

(p. 82, top left)   *Carving intricate motifs*

(p. 82, top right)   *Threading beads*

(p. 82, below)   *Dayak sacred animals (a hornbill and a lizard)*

(p. 84, p. 86, top, p. 87, left)   *Ornamental motifs of the Dayak Kenyah tribe*

(p. 87, right)   *Ornamental motifs of the Dayak Bahau/Modang tribe*

(p. 86, below)   *Ornamental carving on a rooftop*

(p. 88)   *Boat on the river*

(p. 89, top)   *Mosque on the side of the river Mahakam*

(p. 89, below)   *The Mahakam bridge in Samarinda*

(p. 90)   *Shaman*

(p. 91)   *Playing Gamelan*

(p. 92, left)   *The provincial Government building in Samarinda, where the Governor has his office*

(p. 92, right)   *The Great Mosque in Samarinda*

(p. 93, left)   *Longhouse of the Kenyah Dayak tribe*

(p. 93, right)   *Welcome arch of Samarinda's Temindung airport*

(p. 94, left)   *Benuak Dayak's dancers in Tanjung Isuy*

(p. 94, right)   *Marching*

(p. 95, left)   *A young Dayak girl from the Mahakam interior*

(p. 95, right)   *Marching band Marshal dressed in a Dayak costume*